THE MORRIS FILE
VOLUME 2

The Morris File

VOLUME 2

A collection of works by

ALBERT MORRIS

illustrated by Stuart Macgregor

THE SCOTSMAN
and
G.R.F. SUTHERLAND & Co.

Copyright ©   The Scotsman Publications Ltd.

ISBN 0 902670 05 0

Originally published in book form 1986

by The Scotsman, 20 North Bridge, Edinburgh
and
G.R.F. Sutherland & Co.

Typeset by Waverley Graphics Ltd., Edinburgh.
Printed by Ivanhoe Printing Co. Ltd., Musselburgh.

Contents

Foreword

ONCE, in the dear days, almost beyond my recall, when I had more hair on my head than I have now and when a third edition of my chin had not been published—at the back of my neck—my then editor, Mr Alastair Dunnett called me into his room and put forward a simple proposition to a simple journalist: "I am going to give you a column," he said expansively, as one would offer a suitable residence to St. Simeon the Stylite, who spent 36 years of his life on top of one as a pillar of society thinking lofty thoughts while shooing away pigeons.

To say the cosmos reeled at the announcement would be an exaggeration but I thought I felt the earth move, although it may just have been a slight dizzy spell brought on by thought of all the travel and expenses that running a column would entail.

That vision was quickly dashed when Mr Dunnett, having established that I would be able to adjust to columnar altitude with its rarefied air of authority and verisimilitude, said roundly: "You can go anywhere you like as long as it is no further than Musselburgh and you can spend as much as you want provided it is not more than thirty shillings,"—or say a cool 150 pence in to-day's Comic Cuts' currency.

I faced the issue squarely. It was a good offer. I was not likely to get a better one in a lifetime or writing in the highest realms of journalism, so we shook hands on the deal and I left, not only wondering how to fill a daily space in the paper but—more important—how I was going to spend all that money and where I should go to broaden my mind and columnar width with travel to places that might include such exotic outposts as Edinburgh's Sighthill or even salt-rimed Granton.

I need not have worried. I ventured, greatly daring, to outposts like Bo'ness and Burntisland and even as far afield as Crail—such is the magic wand effect of the wave of a columnar pen—and although I did get to some more prosaic places like Israel, Zimbabwe and Russia, I always regard travel with great caution, taking all possible precautions about personal safety and expense before making a safari, say to a settlement like Glasgow, to study the city's eco-system and its entertaining and educational wild life.

There was also little need to worry about columnar subjects to write about. Mr Dunnett would invite me into his room of an evening to chat about life in general and the column in particular and since the man had a sense of humour that appealed to me, as mine seemed to appeal to him, we would emerge sagging with laughter, I refreshed with new ideas—but with not an extra penny to show for them—and he, doubtless firm in the knowledge that he had helped to prop up a columnar carrier in much the same way that Scots Porrage Oats are said to do for a faltering caber tosser.

Writing a column brings one close to a variety of readers, some persistent correspondents who unfailingly and helpfully point out what they see as grammatical infelicities and blatant solecisms and which are often the result of the column's hard-working and dedicated Error Overlooking Department which also deals with the delicate craft of infinitive-splitting and the fusing of participles.

I have had readers say that while horse-whipping was too good for me, they would not seriously object if I were sent over Niagara in a spiked barrel.

On the other hand, many readers are kind enough to say that my writings about my all-in-wrestling, gasping grapples with life have made them reconciled to their own and while others have revealed that a daily dose of double-strong Morris before breakfast makes them feel gloriously light-headed and as if they were bouncing on a trampoline, other shrewd citizens, whose medical opinions I respect, believe that essence of Morris taken before bed sends them off into a dreamless sleep, with no noticeable side effects, and make the whole pharmacopoeia of sleeping pills seem, in comparison, like nerve stimulants.

While I would like, especially, to thank Alastair Dunnett for giving me the chance to write such a column, I must once again express my gratitude to all those who have helped me get facts together for slotting into sentences for some journalistic Gothic-Rococo piece that may pass all under-standing. Once more I thank all heroic sub-editors on "The Scotsman," who groaned, like galley slaves over their oars, when another File landed on their desks and the hard-working, ever-cheerful and helpful members of the office library without whose help I might have been deprived of vital information life-support systems.

I thank all readers who have written to me in terms of unalloyed encouragement—especially the man who kept sending me bottles of whisky for years and the woman who threatened to leave Australia and come right home to marry me because she felt then that I needed the support of a strong woman and that she was muscular enough to fill the post—and even those who are my severest critics.

I have the equivalent of thirty bob burning a hole in my pocket; Musselburgh looms sunnily on the journalistic horizon. While health, strength, inspiration and circum-stances permit, I'll just carry on columning.

Also published by The Scotsman and G.R.F. Sutherland & Co.

The Morris File
by Albert Morris
(1985)

A humorous collection of favourite writings by Albert Morris of The Scotsman.
Hugely successful in its first year.

"There is no-one like him for the sonorous rodomontade, the tin whistle blown like a
trombone, the black board chalk squeak made mellifluous. Long may his quill
quiver."—*Scottish Medicine.*

£3.95 nett

Orkney Days
by Christine Muir
(1986)

Christine Muir's wonderfully descriptive writing conjurs up vivid images of the flora
and fauna, the happy life, the seasons, the sky, the sea, of this hard unyielding island,
North Ronaldsay, at the most northerly tip of The Orkneys.

£3.95 nett

Travels
by Hamish Brown
(1986)

Whether on foot or ski, sailing or canoe-ing, looking at pre-historic monuments or
chasing birds and flowers or leaping to the defence of Scotland's shrinking wild lands
Hamish Brown writes with a contagious enthusiasm, with humour and an eye for
beauty. His travels will appeal to all who enjoy the rich landscape and traditions of
Scotland. Many maps, illustrated profusely.

£5.50 nett

1

The great divide

WHEN I was but a little chap, with a heigh-ho the belt and the slap, I used to hold up my hand in class, assume an expression of refined urgency on my newly-minted Edinburgh and district features and would shoot out of the room in a whirr and blur of movement when the teacher said irritably: "Oh very well then but be quick about it."

It was, as ex-pupils will know, a ruse by scholars suffering from a brain over-full with facts, to get a little relief by wandering up and down the school corridors pressing one's nose against the glass doors of other classes, watching education being drilled into resisting minds and enjoying the benison of a little temporary freedom from jotters, ink-wells and teachers' voices continually harrying their charges to take on more knowledge than children felt their minds could reasonably bear.

One of the curious features of such escapades was the sound that hit the ears of the errant pupil as he ambled from corridor to corridor. That was the great Scottish multiplication tables chant, a mantra equivalent to the Buddhist's "om mani padme hum," that promised those who repeated it often enough, a life of ready reckoning bliss in which they were not likely to be hewers of wood and drawers of water like the children of Ham but might rise to the position of chief clerk or clerkess in some respectable office that would not debauch them with too big a salary.

When, at the end of our primary school days, we were

11

urged to go forth and multiply, we were superbly equipped for such a mental purpose, our tables being filled with such cerebral goodies as the answer to nine times nine or even 12 times 12.

Because Scottish education, at least in my scholastic day, was a well-rounded discipline that could make those who underwent it square up to the sternest demands of the commercial, professional and spiritual worlds, it must not be thought that the devotees of division were neglected.

"Divide and rule" was the motto of our arithmetic classes, words which hinted that such an action enabled Britain to hold imperial sway, keep lesser breeds without such knowledge at bay and helped one to achieve a position of prominence in one's occupation over those whose talents did not add up to any dichotomous significance.

Thus, we were made to sweat over all types of division, bisecting numbers both short and long until our minds sagged, our wrists ached and pencil leads became blunt with the straining effort.

Sometimes, and the agony of such experiences is still with me, we were made to come out from behind the stout oaken ramparts of our desks, walk up to the blackboard and attempt to work out a sum in front of the sneering or wondering class so that our skill in chopping large figures up into salami slices or ignorance of the techniques were shown up for all to see.

Long division, I remember, was a cross between a nightmarish labyrinth of figures and a digital minefield in which the slightest mistake in calculation sent the sum crashing to ruin like the removal of one card from a carefully-placed cardboard pyramid.

Occasionally, in a wild burst of despair, I would write

down the first figure that came into my head, irrespective of whether they were relevant or not.

The chalk dust flew as I worked vigorously to produce a farrago of widely-inaccurate calculations. I hoped, however, as I hacked my way through the sum like one lost in a thorny wood, that as three monkeys, according to the law of averages, set to pounding typewriters might eventually strum out Shakespeare's *Love's Labour's Lost* or Bertolt Brecht's *Mother Courage,* I might, given a little time—say a million years—produce a correct answer.

Scottish education tended in those days to expect pupils to move at a somewhat brisker pace and I was quickly sent back to my desk, the teacher remarking bleakly: "Morris, sometimes I think you will just write anything"—a comment that was incontrovertible then and—examining it now—uncannily prophetic.

Eventually, we hacked our way through the longest divisions and came to the shining uplands of understanding, which quickly darkened as some new arithmetic problem was made to loom before us.

There was, of course, no help given to us in the way of mechanical aids and the only chips we knew then were those served up to us in old newspapers or the ones we had on our academic shoulders.

Counting on fingertips was frowned on and could be cut short with a quick flick of the belt, resembling a chameleon's tongue enwrapping a fly. When we worked out the correct answer it was done after hard mental slogging that left many of us weak in the legs as well as the head.

Can it be wondered at then that an old arithmetical veteran like me is not too pleased at the report that pocket calculators and microcomputers were now essential for school mathematics lessons according to a discussion document, *Mathematics from five to 16,* issued by the schools inspectorate.

The document also declared redundant some aspects of traditional mathematics such as long division and logarithms. "Only very basic and simple calculations need now be done on paper," the report says. "Some standard written methods of calculation, such as long division, which many pupils find difficult, and few really understand, should no longer be generally taught."

I cannot be the only one, who not only knows his multiplication tables, was an avid solver of arithmetical problems involving that active trio Messrs A, B and C and finally cracked the hard nut of long division, who considers that statement depressing and defeatist.

I find insupportable the contention that because pupils believe long division to be difficult their intellects should not be taxed with it. Many young scholars must find Shakespeare difficult. Are they to be kept from scaling the bardic heights because it is felt modern youthful minds are too frail to tackle them?

I say to these spineless pupils and equally flaccid educationalists: "Let the long division be tackled with true British grit. If calculators are to be used, it should be made clear how these infernal machines arrive at their answers."

I was in a shop recently where a young assistant failed to give me the correct change even though he used a calculator. At one time any assistant worthy of his hire could have worked out the answer in a fraction of a second.

What happens if our technological super-children do not have a calculator or microcomputer handy to solve some long-divisional problem? I expect they will be found muttering over their hands, working it out with paper and pencil or with matchsticks. It will be as easy as falling off logs.

I hope they get the right answer; three monkeys hammering at typewriters might get it quicker.

2

Around the corruption sale rooms

BECAUSE I know just about everything, many puzzled people have asked me to explain a headline in a newspaper—not this one—which stated: "Prime Minister Orders Fiddles Probe." All wanted to know what such a probe was, some whether it had musical connections or was a technical instrument as used by the Inland Revenue, and others whether it could be obtained by mail order or by a straight cash-across-the-counter purchase.

A fiddles probe, of course, is a device which, though obscure, has a long and honourable history and was used to stem the flow of notes caused by someone too obviously involved in lute-plucking or string-pulling, often in connection with lyres.

A papyrus document first mentions a device of this nature made of greased palm leaves, nest feathers, a backscratcher type handle and some unknown materials being used in the court of Senusret 1, a twelfth dynasty Egyptian ruler, for the scouring of offenders who had struck jarring notes against the slow, traditional rhythms of court practice and prevailing society.

A relief sculpture on a tomb near Wadi Halfa shows this device as a symbol above two figures, one holding an outstretched right hand and placing his left one, palm upturned, behind his back, into which the second figure furtively drops a coin. Hieroglyphics roughly translate the phrase as "Ptah Ptolemy."

Leonardo de Vinci was said to have devised such a probe

for Lorenzo the Magnificent of Florence, based on a now lost principle of hydrodynamics, and another, for Cesare Borgia, which used a lapis lazuli pistol grip and had two slim bronze barrels—on which were painted scenes from the "Battle of Anghiari"—for firing a hail of stone bullets at offenders.

The Elizabethans used these probes with great effect against the "craftie lollie laddes" and the Victorians in characteristic fashion had them wrought in cast iron and brass, many showing morally uplifting scenes of corruption through the ages.

It is good to know that the Prime Minister is taking an interest in such objects which combine artistic excellence with ethical purity and moral probity. She should have been present at a sale at Graftons of Grimness of these and similar articles which created much interest the other day.

Regarded by many as the piece de resistance was undoubtedly the 14-feet-long Bessemer steel and oak fiddles probe made by Warner & Keane of York, 1836, in congealed green, acid purple and unburned sienna with gilt encrustations representing scenes from Victorian life such as peace, war, forelock-touching, male supremacy and the allied occupations of corn and poverty grinding. This was sold—no questions asked—to an anonymous buyer for £47,000.

A bronze, early nineteenth-century vice racket for use with the backhander stroke, and a small wallet-liner made of a type of fleece was sold to a Brig o' Murk business man—no names, no prison drill—for £2480 after some spirited bidding.

A remarkable 1949 Royal Commission carpet, useful for

sweeping findings under, fetched £3500 but a small social compact made of highly-polished impacted waste slag inside of which solemn and binding trade union promises were inscribed failed to realise its reserve price of £170 and was withdrawn.

The highest price—£83,000—went for a 1936 fully equipped with cocktail bar and matching machine-guns Payola, an instrument producing a variety of crisp notes, constructed in double-deal and run with just a touch of the old oil. Buyers were Mafia Holdings of Washington who made an offer no competing dealers felt inclined to dispute.

3

Outposts of British reserve

NO foreigner studying the British public's emotional structure in the seventies could be blamed for supposing that the massive resources of native phlegm were draining away as swiftly as our gold and dollar reserves.

Hardly a newsreel is shown these days without its clip of Britons taking part in some protest demonstration, marching with inflammatory placards, clenched fists and rolling eyes, or battling with each other in football grounds or with passers-by or the police in the streets afterwards.

When not taking part in such passionate social rituals they are—if TV plays, documentaries and the Sunday sensationals mirror life accurately—engaged on pre and extra-marital sex on an impressive scale, wife-swapping, deserting and battering, staging sit-ins, walk-outs, punch-ups and shut-downs, and committing mayhem or worse behind the chintz curtains in quiet suburban streets, where their neighbours always thought they were quiet respectable people who "kept themselves to themselves."

Yet according to Mr Dougal Mackay, a psychologist at St Mary's Hospital, London, the traditional reserve of the British is so acute that some people are incapable of showing even the most basic emotions. He told delegates at the British Psychological Society meeting in York of eight-week courses he offered to "emotionally-constipated" couples, during which they were encouraged to quarrel and then to progress to "pillow bashing" and to work up to anger. The couples are set homework in which they move on to seduction scenes—"anything to help them overcome their terror of showing emotion."

It is good to know that in a Britain that has ceased to be Roman and has become—with no disrespect—Italian, something of the old reserve which helped to win us an empire, still exists.

Mr Jack Numb lowered his evening paper and stared at the woman he believed was his wife, though he never quite liked to ask.

"I ..." he began. "Yes ...?" she queried, as if awakening from some century-old reverie. "Nothing," he said lamely, choked with what might have been a cake crumb or emotion. He blushed with embarrassment and resumed his concentrated scrutiny of his evening paper.

It was like this always. Hilda or Hilary—he never could remember her name exactly, though he noticed she often answered brightly enough to "old girl" or "old sport"—was not much of a help at conversational gambits either.

Yes, he could just about remember a marriage to her, the minister's strangled hesitant tones, the best man tongue-tied with British Reserve 79 Old Crusted Port and collapsing across the top table in a faint or worse just as he said: "Just wanna say a few words," and his bride—what was her name again?—modest and uncommunicative except to ask what his last name was, in the best British tradition. He once, he reflected, had a conversation with her just before the last war about eggs, or it may have been bootlaces. Anyway, it embarrassed both and they never referred to the subjects again.

In the war he had a reserved occupation, which made him even more non-communicative. What he liked best was his morning and evening train journeys to and from the city, the carriages packed with equally taciturn men working out crossword puzzle clues with grave contemplation. In 1957, a man had broken the monastic silence and said to him: "I . . ." "Yes . . .?" he queried uncomfortably, taking his mind off the clue for a three-letter Australian bird. "Oh, nothing," said the man, and the incident was now best forgotten.

Lately, however, he noticed that his wife had been looking at him with a strange interrogative glint in her eyes. "Yes?" he had asked. "I . . ." she began pinkly. "Never mind, old girl," he said reassuringly, looking the other way at the stuffed owl in the glass cage.

Outside the world rocked in convulsions of sex, drugs, riots, traffic accidents, bomb blasts and worse. Inside all was as peaceful as the portrait study of Mr Numb's late father, a non-talkative RN Reservist. "I . . ." again began Hilary or Hilda. "Yes . . .?" sighed Mr Numb. "Oh, nothing . . ." she said. It was better that way.

4

Sound of the Mound

AS a long-standing member of the masses that appreciate the free and often desperate speech which can be heard in that ratiocinative area abutting Edinburgh's Princes Street, known as the Mound, I am rejoiced at the report that the feud between the Rev Alan Cameron, former Grand Master of the Loyal Orange Lodge of Scotland, known as "the Hot Scot" because of his bagpipe-playing and preaching and Mr Samuel Semmens, a lay preacher, appears to have been settled.

As a result of a sheriff court action, the men—both well-known Mound speakers—agreed not to molest or interfere with each other or to make slanderous or defamatory remarks prejudicial to the good reputation of each other.

Although it is, perhaps, sad that recourse to a court was needed to end the oral assaults of the two men, the report of the case sent a frisson of quiet patriotic pride in my contentious city through my Edinburgh-built, all-weather body.

For some time I had thought that the Mound, as Edinburgh's equivalent of London's Hyde Park Speakers' Corner, was going into a decline with only a few featureless opinion-deliverers and true-faith-revealers left to address the wild winds and a scattered band of watchers who had paused by them, perhaps only to fill in the spare time of a commercial day.

It is not so. There is life, it seems, in the old place yet; personality has locked horns with personality, verbal blood

22

has been spilled and the argumentative traditions of that area, which has seen fists and even stones fly, have been carefully maintained.

Although the Mound does undergo a kind of caterpillar metamorphosis into a bright butterfly display during the Festival when the space is often taken up by groups that might include Albanian girl pipers, nose-flute dancers from Upper Volta, artistic mendicants, born-again Bolsheviks, flat-earth disbelievers, cold gospellers and people who believe, against all contemporary scientific thought, that the end of the universe is at hand, it is not the disputatious place that it was.

At one time the verbal shot and shell, priming and powder was as thick perhaps as the acrimony heard and felt at the battle of Balaclava or the charge of the Scots Greys at Waterloo. The Mound was once a seething maelstrom of cloth caps, under which opinions, insults, jeers, rational thought, high-flown philosophy and downright salty language mingled in a noise that was no doubt the authentic voice of British democracy at full bellow.

I remember the childish wonder I had when first taken there by an uncle, rumoured to be a disillusioned anarchist, and who was a keen listener and sharp questioner on many matters ranging from the correct interpretation of *Das Kapital* to the possibility of Marxists being excluded from any democratic life after death.

What a glory for the eye and ear was there. We would join a group listening intently to one man attacking the alleged economic evils of imperial preference and working himself up into a frenzy about very little when I, in my childish judgment, came to sift matters. Then we would drift away, our ears entranced by the siren song of the Salvation Army

singing, brass-playing and drum-thumping a message of
hope for the lumpen, grumbling, misshapen but inexplicably
cheerful proletariat and anon we would offer our temporary
allegiance to someone with flashing eyes and floating hair,
who looked as if he had drunk the milk of paradise and
wanted to talk about it.

There were, of course, favourite performers, whose
appearance would guarantee a flock of aficionados around
them and who would home-in with the alacrity of gulls
about a herring.

These were men—I seem to remember the occasional
woman who tried manfully and not always successfully to
compete against the rumble and thunder of male voices—
who with bright, sardonic piercing eye and tongue that was
wielded like an open razor, mentally eviscerated some
unworthy questioners, cut to size the egos of others and sent
some brazen and presumptuous opinion-exchangers
dodging back into the masses as their views were treated
with the contempt that the crowd and the speaker thought
they deserved.

There was one elderly man, who always caught my
attention because of his stark and tragic bearing. He was
dressed in once smart but then faded clothes and had wild
white hair and rolling eyes that made him look like Lear bated
and scorned by Regan and Goneril and recently emerged
from a particularly storm-tossed part of the script.

He seemed a keen student of the works of Thomas
Carlyle. He always had a battered copy of the author's
Sartor Resartus in his hip pocket which he drew out
occasionally for a long, visual draught, and seemed much
refreshed and strengthened by the action when he snapped
the book shut.

Stuart Macgregor.

I was never very sure what he was on about—it could have been the development of asceticism in the Hindu religion or scepticism about the authority of the Athenian texts of the Homeric poems—and I am sure all around me were equally baffled.

Nevertheless, he could hold the attention of the open-mouthed audience who revelled in the performance, perhaps in the way Russian peasants enjoyed the appearance of holy fools about the countryside.

He raged and reasoned, ranted and roared, spoke, now in a wild, disjointed way, now with intricately convoluted sentences that were broken by long pauses during which he looked sharply at his audience with a blue alcoholic stare as though defying anyone to contradict him.

The extraordinary thing about the Mound was that one was never sure who would be overcome by a sudden desire to bawl his opinions at the wondering world.

Standing beside you would be perhaps some weedy-looking chap with a Wild Woodbine drooping tamely from his lips who would not seem, even at a second glance, capable of raising his voice above a nicotinal crackle and cough, let alone letting the crowd have an earful of choice, freshly-formed opinions.

Suddenly, he would drop his smoking butt, stand on it with a provocative gesture, take a deep breath and boom out his views on anything from support for the International Brigade against Franco hordes in Spain or the iniquities of the municipal administration in Edinburgh, calling our sage and reverend city fathers—as I heard one say—"meal-ticket philosophers."

People would either stand, stare and maybe listen or just drift away and he would be left talking to a brace of uninterested pigeons or a couple of mud-bespattered urchins salivating intently over eroded lollipops.

At that time, people all over Edinburgh and maybe as far afield as Dalkeith and Musselburgh were suddenly starting up, as if goaded by who knew what hidden forces, and with intent expressions on their faces, going, like sleepwalkers, to the Mound and letting fly at the crowds any political or other matter that had been bottled up inside them. The area was a kind of safety valve for the prevention of revolution or uncouth demonstrations on the shopping side of Princes Street.

My uncle had certain views on the alleged perfidious role of Britain in the Russian counter-revolution. Greatly daring, he once cleared his throat and gently uttered a few words that he hoped the world might have cared to hear. No-one paid the slightest attention. Blushing, he raised his hat and walked away. He did not have the Mound sound; Messrs Cameron and Semmens obviously have. Good luck to them.

5

A breath of Fringe talent

THERE I was, in my usual Fringe audience posture, body sagging as it quickly and painfully found out the limited ergonomic possibilities of the wooden seat on which I sat, head drooping as my mind grappled with the elusive emotional, physical and spiritual complexities of the play and tried to bring some cerebral light—however dim and faltering—along the cobwebbed obscurities of the work's socio-political, religio-scientific and psycho-sexual commitment.

It was hard going but we Fringe audiences are made of stern stuff, like an unyielding stern and rockbound coast against which the waves of culture, traditional-comical, pastoral-historical, and historical-spiritual lash themselves in vain. We do not repine or fall into a fit or faint—at least not many of us. In any case, the local viewing element realise that it has paid its money and made its choice—however bad—and it will not be moved, neither by emotion nor crowbars, from its chosen ordeal.

What I like about the Fringe is the whiff of the unexpected that you can get from attending its offerings. At this production I was suddenly jolted into noticing some new and rich sonic effects that were obviously meant to suggest an element of growing menace in a society which helplessly saw its old standards being eroded and changed into something resembling one of the less cheery paintings by Breughel.

The noise appeared to affect the cast in a way that seemed

28

splendidly realistic. Deep breathing, soft at first, but growing heavier by the second until it resembled the snufflings of some great horned beast of Nordic mythology, it seemed to fill the stage, nay the theatre. The cast looked at each other in wild surmise and I said to my companion. "That's good. Heavy breathing, as heard behind doors and in phones. That is exactly the symbol to sum up the rottenness of today's anarchistic society. This is really well done."

My companion, who because of a ticket mix-up was sitting behind me, whispered agitatedly: "That's not part of the play. There's a man beside me, snoring heavily."

Indeed it was. A gentleman well stricken in years who could have played Polonius, King Lear or John of Gaunt— no, or at least very few, questions asked—had, it seemed at first glance, succumbed to the pressures of culture and after the Festival's fitful fever, was sleeping well.

But an old Fringe watcher like me is not so easily taken in. I leaned over to my companion and with the wisdom of theatrical years, was able to explain to her that although the man appeared to have come in from the cold for a quiet kip and was diffusing an unexpected whiff of what seemed like straight gin and creosote, it was very likely that he would get up, utter a statement that would explain all in theatrical terms, and move to the stage, to the surprise and amusement of the audience which would like to be fooled in that way.

"Well, ask him to move now, he's leaning on me and I don't like it," she urged. I gave him a tentative prod and gosh, the astonishing technique of the fellow—he fell forward like a badly-stuffed crocodile across my shoulders.

I pushed him off respectfully and he toppled sideways against a woman who did not appear to appreciate the subtleties of this kind of audience participation. Suddenly he slumped backwards with a completely naturalistic movement bespeaking the polished professional and relapsed into snores that sounded like the war drums of a Zulu impi. By this time most of the audience's attention was rightly on the new actor. "It's straight Stanislavsky of course." I told my friend. "It indicates a psychologically-oriented internal development with great simplicity of external expression. Get it?" "No," she said.

Towards the end, the man sat up, stared around him and said with wonderful clarity: "Ahhh Hmmm," then resumed his troubled sleep again. It was, like Hamlet's "mobled queen," good. When the curtain fell he was still snoring and this obviously symbolised the complacency of today's civilisation surrounded by omnipresent forces of disruption and disaster. I knew all along it was part of the play. You can't fool an old Fringe hand like me.

6

Sepia tint on a sunny day

WHY, we wonder as we stroll along our familiar ways in unfamiliar Mediterranean temperatures, is fate so good to us? The nation is at peace, deep-breathing its sunny bliss. True, the Ruskies are arming at a frantic pace but let us worry about that tomorrow or next week.

At home we may have lurched to the abyss of economic disaster, but with the help of foreign capitalists to aid our Socialist realm we have not gone over. The pound seems steadier, our morale is rising like the temperature and one day—oh, quite soon—we shall get our pot of gold at the beginning of the old rainbow. We are certain to be rich— like we were many years ago when the Imperial flag flew over dominions of palm and pine and the guns of our battle fleet were daunting reminders to the presumptuous of the perils of violating Pax Britannica.

July 1, 1916, it seems, was just such a day of sun, soft air and bird song over Picardy when the cream of this country's young men, the pick of sternly-pointing Kitchener's new armies rose from their trenches on the Somme and advanced steadily into withering machine-gun fire. Fate dealt them grievous strokes and, as that summer sun set on the first day of that famous non-victory, 60,000 British casualties were listed, nearly 20,000 of them dead.

It was all so long ago and indeed, I hardly like to mention it, the weather you see being so fine, and in case it jogs the conscience, and upsets the digestive juices of those who

31

would rather not be reminded of how the British khaki
innocents died on the barbed wire and in the mud of the
Western Front, while songs were sung about them in
parlour and music hall and genteel ladies busied themselves
with white feather distribution and other good works.

I suppose I would not have mentioned it at all—
Wimbledon being on and with so many other things to do
with one's time—except that I found some World War I
family sepia-tinted, faded photographs in a cupboard the
other day.

There they are, the youthful, serious, curiously open faces
of those of whose likeness I bear some traces, dressed in ill-
fitting uniforms of the Black Watch or Argyll and
Sutherland Highlanders or in the nippy well-tailored outfit
of a subaltern in some unknown Scottish regiment.

They are all volunteered. One—an uncle—actually slept
outside the recruiting office in Edinburgh all night so that he
could be first in the queue to join up the next day. There
were so many like them who marched to the front with the
hearts of boys going for some healthy, open-air activity,
imbued with the ideals of the Boys' Own Paper.

The first few days of battle—if they survived—effectively
stripped them of illusions about the glory of war.

I really don't want to go on about this because World
War I and the second instalment 20 years later were really
quite upsetting, and its sure to be another fine day
tomorrow and we all want to make the best of it while it
lasts. But sometimes you can't help pushing back a lump in
the throat when you read about soldiers preparing to heave
a lump of flesh from a trench because it offended the nostrils
and someone with infinite compassion saying:"Easy there.
That was some mother's son."

I do not believe that such an extraordinary convulsion of patriotism on the 1914 scale could ever happen again in this dear old complacent little country. The national psyche has been, I think, scarred for all time by the Somme and similar blood baths, and by the experience of World War II.

We no longer have faith in the invincible general, and our suspicion of the words and deeds of politicians is galactic. This would seem to be true of other countries which took part in two European holocausts.

But let's get out into the sun which shines on you and me, and of course on the graves in Flanders fields. But we needn't think too much of that. Certainly not when the weather is so fine.

7

My big rock-candy Blackpool

I LIKE Blackpool. Well nobody's perfect and I have faults, although not, if you will believe me, many. I am not sure whether liking that breezy, bracing, candy-floss swallowing, bitter-beer belching resort where the collar studs and National Health teeth flash in the sun and where the cloth caps seen on the promenade resemble the background for a painting I once saw of Lenin haranguing the mob, is in fact a fault.

Certainly the dear elderly ladies in my Windermere hotel were mildly astonished when I told them I intended spending a day of middle-aged frivolity in Black (of all places) pool. What, give up even for a few hours, the sublimities of Lakeland where every mountain, grove, stream and lay-by bespoke a deathless memory of W. Wordsworth and his lofty poetic pals for the clamour of the crowds and exchange the eloquent ripple of a mountain stream for the vulgar squeaker? Right on! I regret to say that now and then the feeling comes on me that a short, sharp exhilarating injection of Blackpool into my system is what I must have.

And there she is again, resembling a well-developed Renoir barmaid, the paintwork a bit obvious, a bit battered by time, flashy certainly, but with a style and a smile as she eases you gently of your cash.

Other resorts have not any thing to show more fair. Dull would he be of soul who could pass by a sight so touching in its hilarity. The tower itself, that gigantic Meccano

34

extravaganza that looks as if made of left-over pieces of the Forth rail bridge, which although it is aesthetically galaxies apart, has curiously the same effect on me as the multicoloured, onion-domed, St Basil's Cathedral in Moscow— a distinct lightening of the spirits at such joyous bizarreness.

Despite the brisk south-westerly wind, people are out on the promenade getting their tonic dose of ozone, the majority middle-aged or elderly although there are some youngsters, denim-clad and goose-pimpled, walking as if with bandaged Chinese feet of the old dynasties, on platform soles.

It is the co-operative stores en fete, Coronation Street on sea, a whiff among the deep fry, peas and vinegar and Nivea cream of the Thirties, an evocation reinforced by a group of strolling women, mackintosh and headsquare clad, singing "Daisy, Daisy" with invincible gaiety and with high reedy voices reminiscent of the young Gracie Fields keening over her aspidistra.

Blackpool is geared with impressive efficiency to give people an opportunity to enjoy what is still regarded as a traditional British seaside holiday and the feeling of restrained euphoria is catching. On the Central Pier deckchairs, the crowd, broken down by age, sex and the debility induced by merely living in a world grown more dangerous, complicated and irrational, enjoy themselves, muttering comments and complaints to each other, amid the gulls' cries and the nappy-rash victims' howls.

" 'Well,' I told my doctor. 'Its the pink medicine I need, the one Dr. Frinton gave me when I was bronicle.' But no, he never listened and he just gave me them tablets and told me to keep off pastries and white bread."

"So I said to her: 'It's your life, Lorraine. You're over 16 and if you want to make a fool of yourself with a married man you've only got your own bed to lie on.' " "Of course the lining came right off my stomach. That was before my husband left me and I had to live on milk for three years. I was never the same afterwards you know." "The specialist said it wasn't a varicose vein but anyone can see that it is. Look (displaying a curvaceous female leg with vein markings resembling the surface of Mars), of course it is. 'Don't be a fool,' I told him."

A female fortune teller pointed a regulation talon-like finger at me and said: 'You're not appreciated at work and there's some is jealous of you but you'll arrive at a position of great responsibility before long or you'll know the reason why. You're also far too generous with your money and there's those that take advantage of it. You understand, love?" I understood, paying her a small fortune of £2.

I can't help liking big rock-candy Blackpool. I have a soft spot for it even though it centres mainly in my wallet.

8
Longest sentence

THE columnar day was in full pendulum swing and the young—well, middle-aged— onlie begetter of creative works in this deep space was at his place, chipping, hammering, moulding and hacking at a sentence which, when knocked remorselessly into shape, would form a group of words, elegant in form and impactive in meaning that would burst in the mind like shrapnel, the vibrations of which would linger on in the subconscious, perhaps with a half-life of years.

Miss Angela Primstone, chatelaine of the columnar wine cupboard, was polishing a bottle of rare Albanian claret, once the property of the former Hungarian royal house, and various lackeys dashed about their menial tasks with good humour, some touching their forelocks or curtseying, and some doing both, as they passed the massive Gothic-Scottish-baronial-rococo-type bog oak desk on which I produce raw columnar thoughts for processing and onward transmission to the page.

In short—though that may not be the best description— it was a typical hum-drumming, run-of-the adjectival mill day, with the verbs particularly passive and neatly stacked in nominative cases, that is typical of work in the columnar precincts. Suddenly the peace of our minds was shattered by the abrupt arrival of J.C. Feeney, chief typographical error overlooker of this space.

The man was upset. I could see that but tried not to be influenced by his feelings. "Well, Feeney," I said affably, "stand up straight, chin in, chest out, feet together, hands by your side and say what you have to say."

A chap like me knows how to handle one of the masses. If I had been in St Petersburg during the Russian revolution I am strongly of the opinion that the sans culottes—or whoever they were—would not have stormed the Winter Palace.

Feeney seemed not to notice my words that were calculated to put the fellow entirely at his ease. He shoved a copy of last Friday's column in front of me and said in a voice that shook with eloquent proletarian rage. "There is a sentence here that is 148 words long. The men, some women too, are getting restive. A few of the lasses fainted at their work being unable to take in sufficient breath to get through the sentences in one labial, if you will pardon the expression, fricative go, an apprentice went down with asthma shortly after reading the sentence and another is complaining of inflammation of the gerund and making a noise like a hen with hiccups.

"It's got to stop, Mr Morris. McEnemy, the chief comma adjuster and semi-colon caulker of the No 2 Blohm and Voss, flat-bed, triple-expansion, paragraph-production plant, says that any more of these sentences and the main columnar bilge pipe will crack and ratiocinative pressure fall from over 1,000 to 24lbs per square inch."

There is many a tale I could tell of the old imperial days when I was in the Royal Army Mobile Stationery Corps and, under conditions of extreme strain, kept the red administrative ink flowing to maintain the healthy Mercator-projected hue of British possessions in lands of palm and pine. I was therefore in a position to adopt a calming approach to Feeney, one of the more excitable kinds of Celt.

"You must understand," I told him, "that a long sentence is not necessarily a bad thing. I try to construct sentences that have the effect of a slowly gathering wave that gradually, and with many false crests, works itself up to a towering, terrifying mass of liquidity and crashes against the grim, black-browed rocks of readers with a majestic surge and thunder that I might compare to the Trojans breaking the Greek ranks and sweeping all before them even down to the boat-flecked beaches."

"I . . ." said Feeney. "You must remember," I said, "that there is a certain cadence, melodic line, sonorous quality and impact in a long sentence—read your *Decline and Fall of the Roman Empire*—that is entirely lacking in the banal stacato of a short one. It could be the difference between *Baa Baa Black Sheep* and the choral part of Beethoven's 9th Symphony."

"Well . . . " interjected Feeney but I seemed not to hear him. "A long sentence could also be likened to a kind of intellectual cataract, a literary Niagara, that sweeps all cogent thought before it as if it was a matchstick. Many readers like such sentences and behind closed doors practice writing them. Some have been sent to me, a few minus all efforts at punctuation, and have reached well over 100 words, not including the 'hoping this finds you in the pink as it leaves me at present, and I have given such enthusiasts columnar encouragement."

"You . . ." put in Feeney for some reason. "I am not against the short sentence," I continued, "indeed have often used it, but to get the full flavour and thrust of many of my thoughts, a sentence of not less than 36 words and certainly not more than 1,000 would seem to be about right."

"Just a min . . ." retorted Feeney. I thought the man was

beginning to get my drift so I continued. "You will see then that a mere 148 words to a sentence is a bagatelle. Why, I once counted a sentence of 230 words, including six brackets, written by a B. Levin somewhere.

"Even that is as a gnat's sting to a rhinoceros charge when compared with the sentence of 1,300 words that appeared in *Absalom Absalom* by William Faulkner and one of 3,153 words in the *History of the Church of God,* written by Sylvester Hassell of Wilson, North Carolina, US in 1884 which had 86 semi-colons, 390 commas and masses of readers clutching their throats all over the land of the bounteous word and gasping for air."

"I may say," I told Feeney who was by now backing to the office door with a wild look in his eyes, "that the longest sentence to have got past the editor of a major newspaper is one of 1,286 words in the *New York Times.* It was written in 1981 by one of the giants of the art, Herbert Stein, a man to whom I raise the Morris columnar sentence in salute.

"Not so fast," I told the columnar minion who was making strange bleating noises and clutching at my elbow in a piteous manner," and you will hear that the report of the president of Columbia University 1942-3 contained a sentence of 4,284 words and that the first 40,000 words of *The Gates of Paradise* by George Andrzeyevski appear to lack any punctuation and must therefore be taken to be one grand, glorious sentence like the sound of a great amen."

I asked the veteran error overlooker if I had convinced him of the rightness of my views. "You have, Mr Morris, by the simple and honest nature of your remarks, indeed shown me the true wisdom of your views. I will go and inform the workers," he gushed, lurching into one of the corridors of power on which the great tread, "and I am certain they will receive my words warmly."

Ten minutes later, I was on the speaking tube to the men of the massive sentence presses. "Raise the word total to 237," I said crisply, insert seven commas, two colons and let the column rip." An anwering cry rang merrily from the syntactic depths and once more, the columnar day was back on even keel.

9

Pack up your noodles

ACCORDING to a report, the British soldier's culinary tastes are much improved compared with say 20 years ago. He is, it is said, on the way to becoming a gourmet. For "old sweats" kept in prime battle conditions on bully beef, Irish stew and NAAFI buns, the Catering Corps cookery book, which contains over 1,000 recipes, would seem something in the realms of fantasy.

The scene is a section of territory near the small German village of Bad Oder held by the 1st Battalion, the Queen's Own Digestibles, nickname "The Gastronomes from Hell," regimental motto *in vino veratis*.

An early warning sounded by the brigade headquarters' latest infra-red electronic cooker had alerted the canteen-hardened men that across "no-man's land" Ivan was cooking something and that pretty soon the grim-faced Russkies, with soup-stains on their uniforms and, maybe even worse, stale bread crumbs on their boots, could start flinging everything—Egon Ronay knew what—but the kitchen sink at them.

The situation was tense and had been simmering on a low light for at least 12 hours before being brought to the boil and Capt Harry Cracknell of "B" Company, despite the chill dawn mist, perspired slightly like a toothsome piece of fine old English cheddar.

In the air was the scent of impending struggle, the smell of curry powder, the grapeshot whiff of garlic, the terrible reek of leek and the lingering scent of Yorkshire pudding and tripe, the last two designed to stop the Soviets in their tracks and have them reaching for special breathing apparatus and anti-acid pills, though not necessarily in that order.

These were stirring times and the captain, straight out of the domestic science division of Sandhurst, with the tell-tale "rookie" oven burns still on his hands and the condensed milk hardly dry on his lips, was as jumpy as a test spit on a griddle.

He uncovered his officers' issue .303 cookery book containing 530 quick-fire recipes, designed to have an enemy—maybe even a friend—writhing in agony five minutes after eating one and looked along the line of his men. It was a reassuring sight and warmed, as on a gas ring, the cockles of his heart.

The six-inch, fast-action Kenwood mixer, elegant but deadly, stood ready for action with Corporal Mulligatawny, a broth of a boy, in charge. Nearby was the .300 half-track chopping board (standard NATO issue but nothing was perfect), the squat and lethal self-loading, swivel-mounted, automatic mincer, a battery of long-range, high-trajectory electric toasters and as a last stand—the nearest equivalent to mustard gas—an arsenal of mixed pickles, designed to set off flaming onions inside any of the enemy unwise enough to eat them.

Fumbling the captain prepared a sawn-off standard, heavy-duty, loaf slice for immediate action, determined to have the Slavs on toast if it came to the crunch.

He was watched by Sergeant (Pig) Trotter, a veteran of 100 battles over a hot oven, the man who blew the thrilling and inspiring "cover charge" at the battle of Canal Alimentaire in Belgium in the dark days of 1940 when all Britain was in a stew and who took his revenge on the sauerkraut swallowers when he personally forced five high-ranking Wehrmacht officers to eat British Army field service Brussels sprouts after the capture of St Pancreas, near Villers Bocage, Normandy, 1944.

Sgt. Trotter, who had done porridge at Sidi Barrani, toasted cheese for assault cocktail parties outside Tunis and stewed kippers for officers' messes along the Arno in Italy, was quick to see that the young officer lad could collapse like a souffle and put the men off their nosh if something was not done. He dashed to the emergency field kitchen and in hardly more time than it takes to ask: "Red or white, sir?" was back with a filled tray. "Here, get that inside you, sir," he said with a reassuring laugh that had carried younger gourmet warriors through the hell of watery jellies, collapsed fruit cakes and a thousand curdled peach melbas.

Captain Cracknell gasped as he saw before him a spine-stiffening plate of *Bisque de Homard,* another of *filet de sole bonne femme,* a third of *supreme de volaille Maryland,* "and for *entremets,* as the Froggies say," said the sergeant, "a nice little *omelette flambee,* all washed down by a bottle of Piesporter Goltropfchen or if you like a bottle of champagne, Mumm's the word how we got it, don't let brigade HQ know."

With an expertise born of short but intense practice, the captain wiped the last crumb from his lips. "Needed that, sergeant," he said appreciatively, "don't know how you do it . . . under these conditions."

"It's nothing," said the sergeant, "just what the lads are having themselves and a lot of them are grumbling (bless their little military tums) because there's no *saumon d'Ecosse* on the menu these days or *truite meuniere*. We managed to get both last year from the mess of the Jocks at Bad Knackwurst in exchange for 6,000 crates of our chateau-bottled Mouton Rothschild, 1947, but that stuff is as hard to come by as after-shave lotion in a Red Army detention barracks".

Suddenly, expert noses in the British lines twitched like alarmed Bisto Kids. From the Russian front tables came the acrid smell of battle-order army cooking. "Don't say they're going to chuck impact-explosive meat balls at us," muttered a young sweat, his voice faltering, who had just come back from battle-eating tactics school and knew that the Russians were coarse feeders who would stop at nothing not even substitute potatoes, in their terrible massed assaults on an enemy menu.

"Smell that," shouted young Lt Hilary Peapod. "they're going to chuck *borscht* and maybe stale black bread at us. Command never warned us about this."

A phone rang shrilly: "Captain Cracknell answered it. "Yes sir, we can see their steam rising, and the sun glinting on their ladles. Right, sir, rely on us to put something that'll surprise them in their bellies."

At a word of command, cool and twiglet-crisp a thousand eating irons were unmasked and glittered coldly in the dawn. Sergeant "Jock" Prunestone, i/c Soups and Cold Appetisers, rushed up with his section carrying fragmentation rice pudding designed to make the staunchest Slav eater crack and all along the lines, recoil-less sections of *cote de porc aux beignets de pommes avec choix de legumes,* as well as the homely but stomach-battering haggis—hand-picked from the land of mountain and flood but none the worse for that—stood ready to be served with interest if the red hordes as much as bared their teeth.

A bugle blew the notes of the regimental "sweet service and alert," entitled "Raisin' cain," someone shouted: "Give them *bombes surprise* in their gobs and cold eel in their vitals," a drum beat the *plat du jour,* and once more the British showed that their appetite for war was undiminished.

10
Friends of the column

AS is probably well known and, if not, rest assured I will not flinch from revealing it, this column has been in the past, is now and no doubt will be, a refuge for well-known personalities of the international scene, many of whom have, after a life of turbulence, grandiloquence and danger at the helm of some country, now perhaps under a revolutionary administration, found useful if not remunerative employment working in a menial capacity to help fill this space.

I have never had it satisfactorily confirmed that Nicholas II, last Tsar of all the Russias, actually filled a post in the oxymoron and litotes flat-bed pressing shop for a short time after this column was started many years ago but there were persistent rumours emanating from the prose purpling shop stewards' canteen that a bearded, sad-eyed little foreign chappie with, despite his oil-stained overalls, a strangely autocratic air and answering to the name of Fred N. Romanov in elegantly-modulated English with just the hint of an ancient Muscovy accent, was in fact Nicholas himself, thought by many to have been disposed off by the Bolshevik canaille in Ekaterinburg.

I never actually met him myself but watchful acolytes used to tell me that he was often observed at regular union-negotiated lunch and tea-breaks sitting by himself and eating Beluga caviare "pieces" taken from a heavily-jewelled sandwich box by Faberge that showed painted scenes from Russian history such as the humbling of the

47

boyars by Ivan the Terrible, Peter the Great pulling teeth from the mouths of countries as a rich Slavonik joke, and the dispatch of 40,000 Russians from Murmansk in the First World War to march through Britain with snow on their boots to boost the morale of the faltering Anglo-Saxons. He disappeared one day as mysteriously as he had come, but before he did so he was often observed in the purple twilight gazing through a window towards the star flecked east when his finely-honed features would tense as if in pain and when he would, as to the manner born, curtly refuse an aspirin or stomach powder from a sympathetic centeen worker used to such facial expressions on the staff.

I mention the distinguished nature of my staff merely because of a preview to an article entitled: "Hitler in Liverpool?" in the "Guardian."

It states: "Last year Beryl Bainbridge wrote a book about it. In Thursday's 'Guardian' she reviews the memoirs of Bridget Hitler, the Irish lass who met Alois Hitler at the Dublin Horse Show in 1909 and married him. Later his shabbily-dressed artist half-brother Adolf came to stay. She waxed his moustaches. 'I set him in the right direction but then didn't he go too far?'."

I cannot of course speak for Bridget but it is just possible that a man, believed to be the former Reich Chancellor himself and who therefore did not perish in the Wagnerian horror of Berlin in 1945, actually went as far as the land of mountain and flood and worked on this column as a part-time umlaut inserter in the early 1970s before our staff-screening and political-filtration security departments were set up. He was drawn to my attention because his strange habit of goose-stepping about the sensitive verb deactivating machines and singing marching songs of old Prussia and the Tyrol in a wheezy baritone was upsetting the apprentice gerundive setters. Despite my stern warnings to have "no more of this nonsense here" his only reaction was to spring to attention, give me an upraised-arm salute, offer me selections from "Mein Kampff" in Portuguese and say that the fatherland needed more men like me.

Before he left my employment "Addy" Hedler as he was known was popular for his ballad recitals at the local British Legion hut, and while he did not share his supposed half-brother's love of horses, he was a popular figure for a time at the Scottish Kennel Club's annual show and at Crufts, breeding and exhibiting the little-known smooth-haired Silesian eel-hound. His Fafnir Twinkletoes III took second in the puppy class at Birmingham in 1972. When he left us that year—to take up, he said, work in a NATO defence-security printing establishment in Rotterdam—many speculated as to the identity of the disturbing stranger who had a strong resemblance to an ageing Charlie Chaplin, but Mr J.C. Feeney, chief overlooker of the typographical errors department, never had any doubt. "It was the Fuehrer himself all right," he said. "Fancy him keeping it dark like that. Of course we thought it a bit queer him playing the French horn in pubs so well and taking a drop of snuff in his beer when he thought nobody was looking, but come to think of it, a lot of people do that in this city."

Of all the people of note who "clocked in" for this column and that includes Dr Milton Obote, former president of Uganda (African affairs department) America's General Westmoreland (columnar global strategic office), the late Patrice Lumumba, Lord George Brown, Dr Henry Kissinger

who often drops in to give me advice—not that I take it—
on matters of high international columnar policy and the
former King Constantine of Greece (high society news), no-
one caused more trouble than the employee who turned out
to be Mártin Bormann, one of Hitler's right-hand men
whom the "Daily Express" has spent millions of pounds to
track down and may indeed still be searching for.

Bormann, under the pseudonym of Alfred Pindrop, was
first employed as a deputy sentence fitter (grade III) in the
paragraph construction shop where he soon distinguished
himself by his superior powers of organisation and the
peculiarly long-winded and Teutonic construction of
sentences; traces of his handiwork are still to be seen in the
column even today.

Always popular at office dances, he was runner-up in the
columnar social club's spot-prize exhibition paso doble in
1973 and was second (partner Miss Elsie McElbow) in the
over-50s military two-step. Although he spoke with a thick
Germanic accent, he soon picked up the more refined tones
of Edinburgh and sometimes could even pass, if the wind
direction was right, for a native.

Bormann—we were never in doubt about who he was—
left us suddenly one day, eight car-loads of "Express"
reporters and photographers in hot but vain pursuit. The last
I heard of him he was working on that paper, masquerading
as a high production official and charming trade union
leaders with his winning ways and disarming smiles.

My only regret about my distinguished employees is that
the late King Farouk of Egypt did not breathe this column's
refined air but had he lived and was able to turn a sentence
or two, who can doubt that a suitable place would have
been found for him.

11

My gift to the nation

WHEN I read somewhere recently that private citizens, believing that the country needed help "in the present situation" were donating sums of money as gifts to the Treasury, I was stricken with guilt, remorse and the feeling that I had been lacking in patriotism.

Somehow I didn't think that Mrs Thatcher would accept charity. She'd be too proud and would even be a bit hurt if someone tried to slip, unseen by her, a £1 into her handbag or sent it to her by post perhaps wrapped in the latest offer from some book club.

Not for nothing have I been a Wolf Cub, a gentleman ranker in the British Army and a purchaser in my time of Government securities, including the dread, irredeemable, War Loan. As soon as I learned that the Government was a bit short and was prepared to take a bit of the ready even from the likes of me, I went to the place where you hand in such things.

The man behind the counter looked up in a startled way, recognising at a glance, the man who, by way of protest against successive British Governments, had handed in the GCE, Army General Service medal and Wolf Cub woggle.

"Not you again, sir?" he asked stifling manfully a slight groan that had sprung unbidden to his lips. "What is it you want to hand in this time—driving licence, smallpox vaccination certificate, Royal Society of Arts shorthand

51

pass scroll of honour or Army discharge papers? Don't hesitate, sir; we'll take anything here, store them nicely and then if you've decided to end your protest, we'll give you them back just as if you had never handed them in."

I smiled first a little smile. This good man was in for a surprise. "I have come," I said, "to give the Government a little gift of £1 to help tide them over a difficult period in their lives."

The man stared; surprise racked his ex-military, ramrod-straight body and he seemed to be speculating on whether his ears had deceived him. "You want to help the government," he asked, "just like that, straight, no questions asked, no names and presumably no pack drill?"

I nodded modestly. The man had understood me perfectly. "There is no need to mention my name but if you feel like giving a hint to some relevant official that it would not come amiss on an honours list with some nice initials after it like KBE, OBE or MBE or maybe something a little higher that not many people might want, like a peerage, I would not object for too long but I rely on you to put it the right way."

The man licked the lead of his pencil and wrote down my particulars. "Don't feel you have to suggest an honour," I said, as he busied himself with the pad, "it's just that so many people I know have one now, including the office cleansing operative and the milk boy that I feel a bit out of things, a kind of outcast, a pariah, maybe even a leper; do you see what I mean?"

The man looked up and said: "I think I know the feeling exactly, sir. It's like a kind of hollow ache in the pit of the stomach. I had that when a couple of junior clerks in here got the MBE, but the feeling went when I became a Knight Bachelor; the relief was instant, overwhelming and lasting."

I forced myself to return to the subject of the money. "You don't think £1 is too small, do you?" I'm willing to give £5 if it would make Sir Keith Joseph feel better and look happier in his efforts to control the money supply."

The man grinned and said he thought £1 spent wisely by the Government might make all the difference in helping the recession to bottom out, cut unemployment at a stroke and deliver a death blow to inflation.

I took the note out of my wallet where it had been comfy and warm and said: "Before I hand it over, there are one or two little stipulations that must go with this gift. I want it to be used to take the steam out of the economy, or to put it back, whichever is more suitable at the time."

"A good idea, sir," said the man, "I'll make sure the Chancellor of the Exchequer has these alternatives clearly set out before him." Somehow I was not satisfied with the assurances I had been given. "You will use this money sensibly, won't you?" I said. "You can spend it freely but not on inessentials. If I find that you've been reducing the pressure on domestic demand with my money when you should have been putting purchasing power back into the home market, I shall be extremely annoyed and might ask for my cash back."

The man, I thought, paled under his ex-serviceman's tan. You wouldn't do that sir," he said. "That could topple the government, send the stock market reeling, depress the Financial Times Index and only encourage foreign speculators."

Oh well, since he put it that way, I was prepared to let the government have a fairly free range with my cash that had been earned by the sweat of my ideas and the pucker of my brow. "Rememember this," I said, "I am not giving this money to pay for an increase in imports and to accentuate the flight of sterling to countries abroad. I want it to be kept here, saved perhaps, or invested wisely in British-to-the-backbone organisations like British Leyland or British Rail. Understood?"

The man nodded. "If everyone was as altruistic as you sir, this country, if I may say so, would not be in the position it is today but that it is only my opinion of course."

I was pleased; the fellow seemed to recognise quality when he saw it matched, as it was, with financial quantity. "Another thing," I said as the man started a third page, "I don't want the money given to pay for the Trident missile system; if it has to be used for defence, I want the lads in the Navy to benefit. Wasn't a Navy-man myself but I have always been an admirer of Britannia's bulwarks along the main and as a child I invariably had a fleet of toy boats in my bath so that shows you how I feel about protecting our island race."

"Very good sir," the man said and asked: "Could we put a little of it towards the development of the Tornado, the multi-purpose, all-weather, highly-expensive NATO fighter, I'm certain the RAF would be touched and gratified by your gesture." "Oh, all right," I said, "and maybe you could see that the Army has a bit as well, especially my old lot, the Royal Army Mobile Stationery Corps."

The man went on writing and then sudden dread struck my troubled mind. "Are you sure giving you this money might not make the situation worse? I have just realised that the pound is extremely strong at present and that is damaging our export markets. Logically, I suppose, if there were fewer pounds around they would do a lot less damage than the muscular masses we have got now circulating about Britain and in countries abroad."

The man laid down his pencil and gazed at me in what might have been awe mingled with admiration. "You could have a point, there, sir. What do you suggest?"

I put the note back in my wallet; I'll either tear it up or keep it by me until I see how the state of the economy is by this time next year.

As the man looked at me, his face worked strangely and I am not sure if tears did not form in the piercing blue of his eyes. "Mrs Thatcher, Sir Keith and all that lot will be very disappointed not to get your cash," he said. I didn't want that to happen, so I thought of a happy alternative to bring the smiles back to their careworn faces. "Tell them I'll try to send them food parcels and some cast-off clothes next Christmas and that they are not to bother to reply; a patriot you see, needs no thanks."

12

The people's ape-man

I have always had a soft spot in my heart—and some would say my head—for the monsters of the screen and popular fiction. Sometimes extremely large, often a make-up artist's miracle in their hypnotic hideousness and usually motivated by all-too-human emotions such as hunger, lust, ill-temper and a mindless desire for destruction, they stalk the movie-screens of our mind and faded films on TV, grunting, howling, tearing, slobbering and accidentally flattening what we call civilised life.

When not eating soft-centred humans as a light but nourishing snack or snapping them like twiglets at a cocktail party, they turn on them a breath of such excoriating power that the effect is like a flame-thrower.

For me King Kong—I refer to the excellent 1933 screen version—will always be the archetypal monster, who, because of his size, occasional burst of irritation, about very little when you came to sift matters, and infrequent, though effective, interludes of free-lance urban demolition, was widely misunderstood even by the caring, sensitive, society of America in the thirties.

As the late Marilyn Monroe said in *The Seven Year Itch* of the creature from the black lagoon: "He only wanted to be loved." Just so. The giant ape fancied—who could tell why?—Fay Wray, a chit of a slip of a girl with an 18-carat heart and a one-carat mind, size four-and-a-half in shoes and 27 in screams.

The half-man, half-fish, an interesting mutation who

could have had a big future in marine salvage work, undersea warfare or helping to raise the *Titanic*, was up to his cleancut gills in splashy and bubbling passion for the affections of an eminently forgettable female, white, Anglo-Saxon, probably Protestant and as interesting as a piece of swamp mud.

Such a mixed marriage—assuming that was what the creature was aiming at—would never have worked, she with a stern Calvinistic approach to life and especially to the tangled obscenity of a South American jungle and he, though he had obvious hidden depths, never fully plumbed, was probably to judge from his somewhat unsubtle, underwater approaches, a primitive methodist from whose eyes the scales had not yet fallen on the imperfections of homo sapiens. There would also be the cost of keeping him in ants' eggs and the labour of changing his bowl daily when they were back in the land of the free.

I have always had a certain sympathy too for humans who got turned into walking carrots—ill-tempered ones at that and who could blame them?—as a result of an encounter with a space germ. Life in future may be just like that with humans and creatures looking like shop-window displays of fruiterers, mingling uneasily and creating obvious problems for some Species Relations Board.

I could never bring myself to dislike entirely Mr Hyde in the novel by Robert Louis Stevenson. I have always felt that in his case the attention of a sensitive psychiatrist and perhaps a couple of dedicated, and at times, nimble, social workers would have fined-down some of the coarse robustness of the character and even slowed-up his hyper-activity.

It is, however, the alleged real-life monsters that arouse

my greatest sympathy. Somewhere, as we all know, in the Tibetan foothills, on mountain sides and in hidden valleys, is said to lurk the Yeti or Abominable Snowman, which, although it has never been seen by a European has left tracks in the snow measuring up to 12 by six inches.

The creature is thought to be either an ape-like man or a man-like ape. Whatever he is, he seems highly skilled in keeping clear of humans who want only to establish an on-going, meaningful, open-ended relationship with him, perhaps taking him into the best society in the way that King Kong was socially introduced to the cream of New York theatre-going audiences.

In many parts of the world there are stories, some whispered over remote wilderness camp-fires, discussed on television with appropriate tantalising, seconds-long, camera shots, related fearfully in some snow-swept, wind-grieved, Himalayan hovel or hiccuped drunkenly in a frontier settlement bar, of strange creatures resembling mankind that are about six feet tall, have thick, red, hair all over their body and unusually big feet which would fit snugly into violin cases.

The latest report comes from China where people are said to have had quick glimpses of such beings, as if seen in the corner of the eye, and where interest in man-like creatures, not yet taken into the fold of the glorious Chinese Peoples' Republic, is growing.

In 1976, it was reported that a peasant woman was chased by such a creature, kept captive by it for two hours in a cave and then released with a peremptory gesture, presumably before she was able to have a quiet discussion with it about man's place in a socialist universe and the alleged decline in the practice of dialectical materialism in European Russia.

Stuart Macgregor.

Some years ago, two simple Chinese soldiers were said to have been set on by a party of pleasantly enthusiastic ape-man-like females, had their uniform stripped from their bodies, and raped. That, at least, was the story the broken men told to their hard-eyed non-commissioned officers to explain their prolonged absence from barracks.

It is interesting to speculate on the possibility that somewhere on this troubled earth, communities might live in a kind of Eden innocence, in the remote austerities of Asian mountain ranges, deep in American forests, or in untracked lands of Siberia.

For them there are no thoughts of possible nuclear extinction, rising mortgage rates, the little red book of Mao, secret police, flying pickets, high-fibre diets, noisy motor-cyclists, cholesterol-low food, the need to jog until the head pounds and the lungs ache, test-tube babies and demagogues spouting their idealogies like cocks crowing on a dunghill.

I see them, in my mind's eye of course, drifting pleasantly and peacefully in their furtive existences, always just beyond the reach of mankind, and always knowing, with the deep instinct of the wild creature, that homo sapiens is bad for the health and that contact with him can lead to anything from nervous pulsations in the chest to sudden extinction.

I see the Yeti, as a quiet, contemplative, creature who, deliberately and probably wisely, chose not to follow mankind into the alleged shining uplands of civilisation, but to lead a simple, healthy, open-air life that might well have suited Adam and Eve, living on roots and plants, and having an existence as placid as those of the great forest apes in Central Africa.

There he sits, under the Tibetan night sky, bright with

the glitter of Asiatic constellations which afford him little or no cause for spiritual wonder, watching perhaps a caravan winding its way through some rugged pass.

What would happen if he approached them, making wild and uncouth gestures of friendship? He would, I suspect, be carried off instantly to the local district commissar for investigation into possible espionage activities. Then he would be given a sound Marxist education, coupled with a course in speech therapy and lessons in group consciousness and political awareness, and—for his own good and as an example of a benevolent state—be displayed as a grateful, card-carrying member of the Communist Party; in short, the people's ape-man.

If he does exist, he is better where he is, in the shadows and hidden places of the world. If he watches men struggling through their existence, does a thought meaning "abominable" ever become linked to the alleged heir to the ages? Surely not!

13

Just my type

MANY people have asked me what sort of typewriter I use to pound out my trackless desert of print that is—as is well known—relieved by a few oases of inspiration, dried-up beds of the once fast-flowing rivers Oxymoron and Litotes, badlands of sentences stretching to the horizon and beyond and scrub areas of parched and peeling adjectives on which lie the skeletal remains of winged thoughts that never really got off the ground.

As might be imagined, no ordinary plastic and soft metal modern typewriter made by nimble Oriental fingers and minds would be adequate to produce such a massive and intricate rococo and Gothic column and the management have seen to it that only machines specially constructed by cunning, gnarled artisans from a firm of iron-founders and steel producers, Fafner-Alberich A.G. Nuremberg—no British manufacturer being able to produce metals able to withstand the enormous physical and mental pressures and stress involved in columnar production—are delivered to my desk.

My typewriter, a Wotan Mark III model, built on lines that strangely resemble a mixture of old-fashioned tramcar, pre-dreadnought battleship and a Wurlitzer organ, is of course, hand-crafted, precision-tooled and ergonomically constructed so that I can sit at it with straight back and firm jaw and with my hands hovering and ready to swoop over the keys like gulls alert for prey, a posture of unswerving rectitude that is of course reflected in my unwavering comments and steel-hard opinions.

The keys are in the old Gothic print, with capital letters an artistic riot of intricate design backed by floral patterns, mediaeval landscapes showing Teutonic knights making dragons go down for two falls and a submission, haunted forests and Rhine castles at the windows of which appear the pallid, thin faces of pure Aryan maidens waiting, presumably, for heroic and ardent swains.

Nothing of that typographical flowering, alas, appears on these pages because the processes of modern newspaper production are inimical to such typographical extravagances. The only time the full beauty of the machine can be appreciated by the public is during the occasional visit I allow to the columnar area when visitors are permitted to file past me and the machine reverently and with hushed voices.

Then they will see the intricate but purposeful flying buttresses on the sides of the machine, the twin towers, Gothic in spirit but already tending to the Scottish baronial in appearance, that house the ribbon spools; the castellated area above the keys which lie like lances in rest and on various parts of the structure, copper panels with etchings showing scenes symbolic of deference, abstinence, continence, dedication to the Western work ethic, as well as superb representations of the domestic lives of Queen Victoria, Kaiser Wilhelm II, Tsar Nicholas II and of former European royalty.

They will also hear the menacing sounds of the great, piston-like keys pounding on paper—likened to the approach of an overweight heavy-booted Nemesis—and see the words being formed with the awful inevitability of the writing on the wall. Many visitors have become so unnerved by the experience that they have had to leave, pale and trembling, and vowing to lead a better life.

It was not always thus. At one time, although readers will scarcely credit it, I was given the same run-of-the-sentence typewriters as other members of the editorial staff— machines manufactured in the Malagasy Republic and assembled in Upper Volta though the ribbons were invariably British—and which after the first few tentative attempts at "now is the time for the quick brown fox to jump over the lazy party," shed screws, bits of flywheels and unidentified plastic components.

As office lackeys rushed muttering to cart away the latest twisted and battered hulk of a typewriter from my desk. I used to stare into the bleak, business-like Edinburgh middle distance and sigh for the great old machines on which I learned the typing skill at a commercial college and which this office used to have in the days when a typewriter took about three sweating navvies to lift and could survive, if not an earthquake, at least a direct hit by a 16-inch gun shell.

I remember, I remember the classroom where my typing days were born, the desks groaning under the weight of upright, stalwart, and armourclad Remingtons, Royals and Imperials which, when operated, made sounds resembling the slow, staccato rattle of a prototype Maxim gun.

Beside them were Olivers and Smiths—machines apparently built of best Bessemer steel, heavy brass, bomb-iron, black bog oak, and rubbber, from the House of Vulcan—that not only stood the test of time but that of hundreds of fingers a month thumping their keys, slapping their carriages and pounding the shiftlocks until something suspiciously like sparks appeared to come from the overheated metallic interiors.

Once, when there was a shortage of machines, I was led by a teacher to a dark corner of the class where an ancient typewriter lurked, its keys arranged in high arches that gave it the appearance of a crustacean at rest. It was very old, the teacher explained, so old that it did not have a device to produce capitals but had rows of capital letters arranged in banks, and was inclined to be "a bit cantankerous."

I placed my hand on the keys which reared up like an alarmed tarantula. Hastily, I sat back but the teacher reassured me. "Go on, it's friendly enough. Show it who's boss." So, I did, pounding at the keys with the slow, deliberate actions of a steam hammer and the machine responded with a kind of dry, clacking sound suggestive of a crab or scorpion scuttling over tiled flooring.

There was something beautiful in the action of that machine that hinted of Gutenberg and Caxton painstaking printing presses and also a suggestion of chisel chipping into granite. I parted with the machine, which left curiously irregular type on the page as if it had been stricken with mild palsy, with feelings of deep regret as one who departs from a genuine work of Victorian commercial utility and art.

The other day I was shown a product of the electronic age—a typewriter with a viewing screen on which one could correct spelling, alter margins, change the lay-out of the page including the re-jigging of lines, paragraphs and words, set out beautifully-spaced columns of figures and could be temporary substitute for an office computer which could do all that and of course, a lot more.

A fascinating machine. On it I typed out a few test lines— the keys do not clack but give out a sound rather like small

birds pecking for crumbs—corrected a couple of typographical errors, daringly split an infinitive and deliberately
misrelated a participle.

It may be that one day all journalists will be equipped
with such wonders but I am too sceptical to accept such new
devices readily and too uneasy at such apparent perfection
of production.

I shall, I think, stick to my old machine that makes typing
sound and look as if the process was one as complicated as
trying to transmute base metal into gold. Shift-lock down,
capitals up and thoughts away.

14

Make mine music

AS a music lover, I like to have a well-balanced, daily diet of the most nourishing harmonies available on the radio market or in my record and tape larder.

On any typical morning, I will probably fortify myself with a nice bit of lightly-done Vivaldi, to be followed by some succulent, thick-textured Bach Brandenberg Concerto and maybe, for a chaser—for I like to start the day with a good-theme glow—a small but tasty slice of slightly-underdone Wagner.

If I lunch at home I can be tempted with a sample of thick or clear Suppé and will follow it—if my favourite *plat du jour* is available—with an aurally-appetising snack of William Walton's Facade. Then, should I feel like a post-lunch nap, I will savour the languorous prelude by Debussy, L'Apres-midi (yawn) d'une faune.

Dinner will certainly see me tackling something substantial, enriched with spiritual vitamins and low in the cholesterol of mediocrity like some juicy, ribsticking, Beethoven symphony, out of which I can joyfully suck the thematic and intellectual marrow. After that, a musical trencherman like myself will not refuse a subtle and satisfying sorbet, say a waltz by Glinka, or—the equivalent of strong cheese and biscuits—a stirring march to go with my coffee and post-columnar mints by Kenneth Alford, arranged by Rimmer.

Naturally, I will have a little night music by a favourite

brand composer before I turn in for some deep, rhythmic and, I hope tuneful, sleep-breathing and so the melodious day will pass.

As an aficionado of music—mainly of the classical variety, although I do not scorn other kinds—I have often found it strange that the melodies that act as milestones in my life and which, at an instant can evoke a place, period or emotion, come from the cruder compositions of so-called "popular music."

That phenomenon again manifested itself in my mind when, the other day, I read of the death of Jimmy Kennedy, the composer of such songs as Teddy Bears' Picnic, Red Sails in the Sunset and the Dionysian Hokey-Cokey, a joyous movement often performed at dances when the spirit of sheer anarchistic exuberance broke through the cool formalities of the quickstep, the foxtrot and the Waltz.

The British were singing Mr Kennedy's songs and others by contemporary composers when Hitler's Luftwaffe was unloading high explosives on their cities, when their children were making rude noises and thus lowering the tone of the war by laughing into their gas masks, when the Yanks were reeling at Pearl Harbour and had little to sustain them for a time except light-calibre songs such as This is the Army Mr Jones and I Left My Heart at the Stagedoor Canteen, and the Ruskies were trying to repel the advancing field-grey hordes by bellowing, in mass choruses at them, songs like Cavalry of the Steppes and Sovietland So Dear to Every Toiler, but having, initially at least little effect.

I realise now that it is not so much Schoenberg, Berg, Berlioz or Beethoven who have sign-posted my life musically as the hitherto unknown—at least by me—Mr Kennedy and others like him.

If anything conjures up my childhood days of peaked schoolcaps, worn leather school-bags and, knees under shorts, red with the wind and the rain, it is the Teddy Bears' Picnic, a melody that I have heard soldiers deliver on route marches but with strangely different words.

Now, it conjures up that comfortable, even smug, world for millions in Britain of the late thirties when the economy was improving, unemployment falling and when it was well-known by any amount of experts that Germany could not afford to fight another war, that Italy was all bluff, bluster and braggadocio and that in any case the Royal Navy would continue to ensure Pax Britannica, if necessary with a few well-aimed broadsides from its 15-inch guns.

The Bisto Kids were sniffing the rich odour of distant gravy as if it was a symbol of good times to come. Other advertisements showed pink-cheeked, confident and pleasant middleclass parents offering Ovaltine and other beverages to their pink, confident, children who in turn would produce school-uniformed and gym-slipped simulacra all avid to dip into the tasty treasures of the consumer world.

Uncle Mac was on Children's Hour in London, Aunt Kathleen stood firm in Scotland for Caledonia's stern and wild striplings and in distant lands of palm and pine, grim-faced Britons were holding the outposts against lesser breeds without Cadbury's Cocoa or Wills' Wild Woodbine.

When the Isle of Capri song enraptured Britons, who tended to spend long periods fiddling with their crackling wireless sets to find the BBC and instead got jerky accordion music in ¾ time from Toulouse or massed patriotic choruses from some station in newly-Nazified Germany, I was in the Wolf Cubs preparing for active adult life by becoming a student of the law of the jungle, as revealed in the Mowgli tales.

Akela, who was elegantly khaki-shirted and kilted, resembled a fine-boned, fair-skinned, pure-souled, female as painted by one of the more intense pre-Raphaelites and used to hum that song in a kind of bird-chirp in between teaching us the intricacies of the running bowline or revealing the aesthetic properties of the clove hitch.

The summer evening sun, shining through the church hall's stained glass windows, would light up her auburn hair like a halo and my cub's heart would beat with a simple pure adoration for her that made me, when the long, Kiplingesque evening was o'er, follow her spoor home so that if she were ever attacked by wild beasts or worse, in the soft dusk that I imagine must have temporarily emulated the evenings in that famed isle, I could, if not protect her, at least shout loudly, in childish treble, for help.

While the song South of the Border evokes the immediate years before the Second World War and that sunny Sunday when Neville Chamberlain told us in curiously flat tones that the Hun, in effect, was at the gate, it is the jaunty *We're Gonna Hang out the Washing on the Siegfried Line* that can still make the faded newsreel of my memory flicker with shots of the war-innocent, grinning, faces of the British Army marching through France and giving the regulation thumbs-up sign, an action of unswerving optimism that seems to have disappeared from our national behavioural patterns.

That tune, the ultimate in cockiness and confidence, epitomised the spirit of Britain at that time when we knew that when the Germans tasted British steel, they would, as usual, fling up their hands and shout "Kamerad" or "I vos a waiter at the Ritz."

The song was dropped after Dunkirk and others of a more realistic or wistful nature took its place. Still, it will always mean the early war years for me just as other songs can bring to mind, in a way that literature or painting somehow cannot, a flavour and texture of the times. "Extraordinary," observed Noel Coward astutely "how potent cheap music is."

Haydn in all his melodic glory, Bach in his superb thematic intricacy and all the other great composers who have enriched the minds of mankind will always be used gratefully by me to bathe and cleanse my spirit. They can never illuminate my past as vividly as popular music has done and so I mourn the passing of Jimmy Kennedy who has gone down in the wood of time and I hope is pleasantly surprised.

15

Darkest deskland

I read recently that a person's desk was a sure guide to its owner's personality. A tidy desk with a place for everything and everything exactly alloted to its place, indicated—as well it might—someone who was ambitious, efficient and remorseless in the pursuit of promotion and power.

On the other hand, the person who kept a desk that resembled a cross between a municipal rubbish dump and a children's adventure playground with the drawers filled to bursting point with papers that should long ago have been discarded or filed, as well as apple cores, partly-eaten bars of chocolate and perhaps a pair of long-forgotten shoes, is either one of nature's undisciplined wage slaves, seldom bound to rise beyond the lower levels of office status or is an erratic genius whose motto with documents is: "I file 'em, you find 'em."

Despite the apparent chaos, the latter can, with the uncanny powers of a tracker dog or a water diviner, lay his hands on any sought-after file or paper with only the merest rummage or flick of fingers.

Many desk workers, unless there are stern office rules concerning the tidying of desks after work, tend, in my experience, to allow papers to pile on them until shaky pyramids are constructed which collapse and spill on to the floor when documents are pulled out from somewhere near the base. An orgy of cleaning up and desk reorganisation is carried out which lasts for a few disciplined days until the first unfiled sheet is covered by another and the process starts again.

I have seen desks that were as organised as army barracks, with pens, erasers, scissors, staple guns and paper clip boxes arranged in ranks and files, ready, like guardsmen, for instant office campaigning. I have seen desks that only their owners could deal with since any unskilled attempt at opening a drawer would have resulted in an eruption of yellowing documents, aspirin bottles. National Health teaspoons, plates containing the detritus of meals eaten long ago, eye drops, old theatre programmes and about a gross of out-of-date football pools.

My own columnar desk, an ancient construction—elderly office workers have placed it as far back as the reign of William and Mary although it has Queen Anne legs and the vestigial remains of what might have been a spinning gallery—is one of the features of my room.

Of massive size and built of mahogany, teak, best British oak of naval quality as well as brass, cast and wrought iron, it has been handed—in a manner of loose expression—from journalist to journalist, each one leaving the indelible impression of ownership on it such as a claret bottle ring, caviare stain, champagne scorch, cigar burn and a curious gouge at the right-hand inner corner which many experts in this field of furniture have interpreted as the result of a badly-aimed sword-stroke by a strong-minded, left-handed person, possibly an irate reader.

When pulled down, its roll-top shows an intricately-carved series of what I take to be contemporary life in Britain and the continent of Europe—the Battle of Dettingen and other sanguinary events in the war of the Austrian succession, work-house inmates in England going about their menial tasks with irrepressible humour, workers wrecking Hargreave's "Spinning Jenny" and French peasants, saluting with deep and abiding reverence, some haughty seigneur of the *ancien regime.*

I remember well how I found the previous occupier slumped over the desk, either from grief at parting with it or from natural journalistic exhaustion at the end of a hard, sentence-constructing day. When told I was to take over, he opened an orb that resembled a bird's eye view of Clapham Junction and said: "Take it laddie with my benison, bottle opener, typewriter eraser, pencil sharpeners and expense account abacus. It is part of the great desk heritage of this country. Treat it with respect and it will reward you with inspiration beyond your humdrum dreams of paragraph chiselling for the public. Don't go into the bottom drawers or you may regret it."

Of course, I was young and reckless in these days when I had hardly a new adverbial clause to my name and I was still paying up for the supply of hard-wearing nominative cases that every writer starting out on a meteoric career ought to possess.

One night, when the only sound in the office was the solemn, slow, ticking of overtime and the heavy breathing of cleaning operatives struggling to brush away spent adjectives, burned-out similes and the fragmented remains of syllogisms and participial adjectives, I entered one of the forbidden drawers and immediately felt a draught of cold air strike me as if coming from some chill, calculating, intellectual force.

A sense of remote antiquity pervaded the atmosphere which reminded me—who could say why?—of that prevailing in the Valley of the Kings in Egypt, a feeling

Stuart Macgregor.

heightened by the cryptic legend written on upper panelling in a precise, literate, hand which said simply: "Make Willie Bauld King of Scotland."

As I explored further what sights met my eyes. I thought I saw 1,000 fearful subordinate clauses that time and use had eroded into fantastic patterns, wedges of unrefined oxymoron, great slabs or rough-hewn litotes that had probably never been exposed for centuries, tangled and rusty heaps of sentence predicates, inestimable deactivated verbs, unvalued examples of meiosis and metathesis, both with a half-life of several centuries, all scattered around me.

Above and below me I saw sentences being formed by the slow drip of the years into long, impossibly-intricate, shapes and somewhere in the intellectual darkness I heard faintly, as a dry rustle, the sound of far-off metrical feet coming inexorably towards me.

I stayed no longer and was glad to breathe the bracing, printing-ink-scented open editorial air and never ventured into the desk recess again.

From time to time however, I have given permission for various philological and semantic expeditions to venture into darkest deskland and present reports to me on what they had seen and heard.

Although all returned safely, many members of the expedition had strange looks in their eyes, especially those who had lost their way and supplies and had to exist for weeks on discarded idioms, husks of intransitive verbs, past participles and fragments of unsaturated polysyllabic humour that had dropped through cracks in the desk.

Some had spoken of seeing grinning skeletons of long-forgotten jokes and others had gibbered of glimpsing and hearing ghosts of ideas that had never seen daylight and were never likely to do so.

One expedition—the great trans-desk etymological trek of 1979—encountered a grisly 230-word sentence that writhed and thrashed about wildly in the shape of a paragraph. It caused a burst of superstitous terror to come from the lips of some of the porters who ran off with their objective cases. That resulted in a shortage of supplies causing the expedition members to live off word roots and pieces of raw, untreated, subjunctive.

Yesterday, I asked Miss Angela Primstone, chatelaine of the columnar wine cupboard and occasional desk duster, what sort of desk owner I was. "Absolutely top drawer, Mr Morris," she replied. She is right, I expect, as always.

16

Wig and a prayer

I WAS standing at my usual bus stop the other day, or rather because of the inclement weather, in the adjoining shelter which the authorities have ingeniously constructed so that it acts as a wind funnel apparently to test the aerodynamic qualities of citizens. My hat, as is the prudent way of bus queuers of long standing, was pulled down hard over my head and my coat collar was turned up so that only my chill nose and spectacles were exposed to the blast.

Despite my cover-up I was immediately recognised. When I cautiously peered from my protective layers, like a wary hermit crab surveying the world outside its shell. I saw that the person who hailed me was an old friend, looking, I thought, remarkably fit and with a head of hair on him that for some reason was only faintly ruffled by the wind.

The last time I had seen him—several years ago—his top covering was much less. Areas of aridity had begun to appear at the crown of his head and the typical peninsular pattern had started to show at his forehead, giving the well-known "noble brow" effect.

By now he might, given the inexorable advance of male baldness, have shown an amount of hair that resembled a small patch of pastureland which an Arab might have tended against the encroaching desert, with a heroic stubbornness and refusal to face reality. Instead, his hair was denser than a tropical rain forest and his brow line seemed to have advanced down to about the centre of his forehead.

78

I commented on his vigorous new growth. He simpered slightly, patted his head with an air of fond proprietorship and said: "I expect you've guessed it's a wig. Got it only last week. Good, isn't it? Makes me look years younger."

Well it did, like a well-haired, slightly-wrinkled, 25-year-old. I congratulated him on his new appearance as well as the admirable limpet-like qualities of his wig in high winds and as he walked and was partially blown away, I mused on the strange coincidental quality of the encounter because only a few days before, I had buried my own wig with the domestic equivalent of full military honours and had shed—why should I hide the fact?—a small silent mental tear as I slipped it into the bucket for the great grim, urban collector that reaps the rich and strange waste of Edinburgh.

I had been rummaging through a cupboard when a cardboard box with holes in it fell from a shelf and out tumbled, like some small furry creature that has missed its footing, the old hair piece that used to go everywhere with me, faithful right up to the moment when I decided not to disguise the ravages of time and male hormones on my suffering scalp, any longer.

I was shocked by its appearance. It had gone grey, a kind of Dorian grey, no doubt because of the effects of its long incarceration and neglect and though it once resembled the faintly-glossy coat of a well-fed puppy—indeed I used to think that if I whistled, it would be bound out of its box, jump on my head and after turning round three times, settle happily—it now looked like a large, terribly aged and scraggy tarantula.

It had to go, but somehow with it, I felt I was disposing of part of myself that had served me with varying effectiveness and although it may not have convinced everyone that I had discovered the secret of combatting baldness, it at least made a few people say that my hair was the best feature about me. It also gave my outings with it a secretive and sometimes alarming air.

To let you understand, as they say in Glasgow, your ordinary wig does not stay on your average head—in the way as a child I believed ladies' stockings were anchored—by some kind of magnetic attraction. Hair pieces are generally fixed to the scalp by a double-sided sticky tape that if properly applied, makes the piece cling to the head as firmly as a limpet onto a ship's hull.

The wig was given to me by an Edinburgh firm that specialised in manufacturing such scalp coverings so that I could write about the experience of wig-wearing and if I wished could be a living advertisement for their products.

I am afraid I failed in that last hope because I tended to run out of sticky tape, tried to make the best of tape that had been used several times—new moorings were always required for each wig fitting—and after a bit the wig would begin to show qualities that were distinctly unsettling and I used to pray inwardly that it would not sever its tenuous connection with me.

It had, I discovered, a tendency to creep along my scalp or give embarrassing indications it was about to leap from my head and onto somebody's lap. These manifestations often occurred when I would be escorting some female to a dance or to the theatre or when I was attending a reception, dinner or party. Sometimes I would put up a hand to still the restless waves and make soothing noises to them, actions that would cause a partner to look at me strangely and perhaps nervously transform pieces of bread into apprehensive balls while she wondered what sort of person was sniffing the sample that the wine waiter had poured and telling him: Mmmm, yes, grand, absolutely. Just pour it now."

Once, on a night of high and vicious winds, I was taking a female cousin to the theatre when I felt the wind rip under the hair-piece which began to rise and ripple on my head.

My cousin kept looking at me as if she could not believe her eyes. "Albert, something strange is happening to your hair," she said. "It keeps rising and falling." I allayed her fears as best I could. "Just a nervous tic," I said. "It comes from overwork and the writing of too-long sentences. It will pass."

In the theatre the wig showed a distinct inclination to transform itself into a beard and began to slip slowly down one side of my head, in such emergencies the trained wig wearer knows exactly what to do. I shoved a handkerchief to my nose. "It's started to bleed," I gasped. I then rose and with one hand in the centre of my face and the other on my head rushed out for a small period of readjustment and reflection on the inscrutable workings of fate and tape.

My kind of unstable wig-wearer knows that windy Edinburgh is inimical to wigs, the air being full of playful or treacherous puffs and that there are certain social occasions, such as Scottish country dancing that, unless the wig is adequately secured with tapes or if the wearer is of a nervous turn of mind, perhaps with safety pins and a piece of cord placed over the head and tied under the chin, should be avoided.

Memory is lurid of the time when, while leaping wildly in either the Duke of Cumberland's Fancy, or the Dashing White Gordon, I felt the wig begin to list to the stern and settle on the back of the head in the way of court wigs when judges, under the weight of evidence, begin to sag backwards on their benches.

To carry on with the dance is a vast mistake and who does so risks the wig sliding from him with an upward tilt like a small hairy *Titanic* in a manner that will do his ego little good.

I gave up wig-wearing after two soul-singeing experiences. One was when an aunt, during a family gathering commented on the rare beauty of my hair and attempted to stroke it. There was a rending noise like a far-off bridge collapse and I felt the wig cling to its foundations only by my desperate will-power.

The other happened on a day of heavy gales when the wig was wind-plucked from my head and rolled along the pavement like a frolicsome ferret. I will never forget the look of sheer pulsating horror on the face of a woman who witnessed the incident. Hair, if you will pardon the expression, raising was the life of my kind of wig-wearer.

17

Hope springs eternally

SOMETIMES, when I see the full moon riding like a ghostly galleon in the sky of pitchest black, when the cold, blue, northern, constellations flicker, and temporarily disappear behind the wisps of flying cloud like Jacks o' Lantern and when the wind sighs softly between the spectral trees, television aerials and picturesquely-wrecked telephone kiosks. I say to myself in a knowing manner: "This is typical Ruritanian weather."

As one who has studied the meteorological conditions in certain works in English literature—areas of low pressure and occluded fronts are a general feature, for instance, of the weather around Wuthering Heights, the country in which Baskerville Hall rears its noble ramparts is invariably given to low evening mists and fitful moaning winds as is the terrain around Castle Dracula—I am familiar with the barometric variations and further outlook of that famous country described by Anthony Hope in *The Prisoner of Zenda* and *Rupert of Hentzau*.

The days in the summer, or what is now vulgarly called the tourist season, are generally sunny and the nights mild as is usual in a Central European country. Sometimes, however, the nights, especially when there is an autumnal tinge in the air can be wind-lashed but with an invigorating tang that often puts people in the mood for vaulting on to horses, galloping wildly in many directions, scaling castle walls and, if necessary, plunging a sword-blade into someone to the accompaniment of mocking laughter.

I see from a correspondence in the *Times* not so long ago, that a reader claimed to have visited Hentzau and described it as "a most delightful spot . . . unsuited to international finance." That was hotly denied by another reader who said that Hentzau had lost its pastoral charm and that nowadays a thick pall of smoke from the chimneys of the State tyre factory hangs over the drab, grey, town.

Foreign visitors, it was stated, were regularly offered as much as ten kropotniks to the £1 sterling, although I believe the official rate is no more than eight. Only a flourishing black market kept alive the tradition of free and often desperate enterprise.

Although a much-travelled man. I have not yet set foot in that land but I have in my possession not only 500 shares in City of Strelsau Tramways (1906) issue at 100 Maria Theresa thalers (old currency) the share but have just received a series of brochures offering holiday package tours in the former kingdom.

Ruritania is now, as is well-known, a signatory of the Warsaw Pact and Comecon and has a landscape of unparalleled interest into containing Gothic moat-surrounded castles that once held kings in their dank innards, haunted hunting lodges and a countryside in which at certain times of the night the ghostly sound of galloping horses, the firing of ancient revolvers and the occasional refined scream of a noble lady in distress can be heard.

It will be recalled that King Rudolph was the monarch of that country, once a junior member of the *Dreikaisarbund,* which became a republic after the First World War, the surviving members of the royal family fleeing to England where the former crown prince, Kevin Oscar Wilhelm Saxe-Coburg Gotha George is the popular "mine host" at the

Sceptreless Crown, Middleman Bypass New Town, in the Midlands. It became a Socialist Soviet State in 1948 after a successful and generally bloodless revolution.

Loophole Tours are offering 14 days in the legend-haunted hinterland (five in the capital Strelsau at the Metropole Hotel, formerly the royal palace) and the rest either in some remote, bird-haunted, wind-shaken castle or *schloss* where excavations often take place to find traces of the visits of English novelists of Victorian times such as tell-tale tobacco pouches, umbrella-cum-swordsticks and evocative remnants of spats and moustache-cups or in the State guesthouse at Bad Oder near the industrial town of Grno famed not only for its modern small arms factories as supplied to the forces of Cuba, Libya, El Salvador, etc., but also for its flourishing government-controlled cottage industry making cloaks, daggers, large, wide-brimmed black hats and face masks of the same colour as used the world over for military or industrial espionage.

Sunstroke Holidays are also "in the picture" with what they call "Living Literature" during which, for 14 or 21 days tourists can go through the literary motions of the two novels and can take part in exciting scalings of castle ramparts, a mid-night swimming in specially-heated moats, three nights in at least two castle dungeons with friendly warders holding the keys and with full nourishing "royal prisoner" board of oatmeal bread in which weevils are fitted with craftsmen's skill, and tonic swamp water.

For those with a good sword arm, foemen worthy of their steel (former members of the Third Battalion, the Ruritarian Rifles) will be on hand to cross blades in a jocular but active manner and take part in the skilled fenceman's rapier-sharp dialogue such as "You fight like a gentlemen, sir." "Yes, my father was the best swordsman in France."

Candle-slicing and tapestry cutting (here only the best Flemish examples showing Boors revelling or slumped in rest and reflection are used) and balancing on battlements can be indulged in when engaging in swordplay while (at special rates) the use of a diving platform for plunging into a germ-free, sulphur-rich, health-giving moat can be had to end a pleasant, athletic and instructive evening.

Also on offer for the history-interested visitor are tours to the State rehabilating centres where members of the former nobility, including relations of ex-Queen Flavia can be shown going about their menial tasks with good humour such as steeping in history articles for the export market including modern ikons and replicas of the gold plate and silverware of the ex-royal family of Rassendyll.

Those contemplating a visit to the People's Socialist Republic of Ruritania should know that Strelsau is a fine modern capital with few traces of the peasant-opressing, grand-duke-foiling, king-imitating city left apart from a few sword-cuts in the oak-panelled reception hall of the former town mansion of Black Duke Michael and the Queen's chambers, now the laundry of the Metropole Hotel, where a faint but evocative hint of some unknown royal perfume still lingers.

The country seat of Rupert in the Schwarzberg district of Hentzau has been turned into a peasants' revolutionary museum and people's cultural centre but it is rumoured that on certain nights a slim, sword-bladed figure looking remarkably like the young Douglas Fairbanks junior can be seen flitting from bust to bust of members of the early revolutionaries, smirking and uttering bursts of ill-restrained laughter.

How to get there: 6.45 a.m. flight from Gatwick or 3.20 a.m. from Heathrow to Munich, there by train to the frontier where tourists will be met by special couriers on horseback to escort the richly-upholstered State coaches to their destination in chapter one of a unique holiday. No correspondence on the holidays can be entered into with the Ruritanian Embassy in London or the State holiday agency (Rurtur). All communications to them are invariably sent back, marked for some reason' "Return to Zenda."

18

Sheltered life

ACCORDING to an advertisement in the *Southend Evening Echo,* a Mr John has informed the public that £3,000 plus VAT can secure any person a place among the 180 available in his converted air raid shelter which will have food and drink for 30 days, a chemical toilet, a video recorder and the use of a microwave cooker.

"Yes," he tells readers. "You will have plenty of time to reach this shelter after the bomb has gone off, subject," he adds cautiously, "to target."

If I were a Southender I doubt whether I would apply to find a bolt hole against the big bang as kindly supplied by Mr John. A thermo-nuclear explosion over Britain would tend to concentrate the minds of survivors wonderfully about what kind of life they would have groping about the atomic rubble and even the use of a video tape-recorder and microwave oven—helpful though they might be—are not likely to be compensatory factors when faced with the breakdown of civilised life.

Apart from that, the idea of being in a shelter again, albeit one with all mod cons like that of Mr John, is not an attractive one to me. I had perforce to be a shelterer for a time during the last global conflict and a lot of my late childhood and early youth was spent trudging with my family to one of our communal hide-outs in the capital when the sirens sounded and the Germans had the nerve to fly over our pure Scottish air and drop their sinister bombs in it.

Although Edinburgh citizens were never partial trog-
lodytes like the Londoners who seemed to spend much of
their existence in Tube stations singing songs like "Knees up
Mother Brown" and the unswervingly dreary "There'll
Always Be An England," they did condescend, especially in
the early years of the war, to sit primly in shelters and
deplore the coarseness of the Teutons and their vulgar
allies.

The characteristic scent of the early forties in Edinburgh
was that of sandbags piled up outside tenement stair heads
and the earthy, damp and raw concrete smell of the air-raid
shelters which were constructed in streets, back-gardens
and drying greens.

The one opposite our house and to which our family was
allocated had been difficult to construct and maintain in a
satisfactory condition since it was built immediately above
one of the underground springs that interlace the well-
watered and verdant constituency of Edinburgh South.

From time to time it would fill up with liquid in which
leaves, branches, tufts of grass and the tiny corpses of
strange creatures or urban garden life floated. Workmen
would come at intervals and pump out the shelter, giving its
interior the dismal and damp look of an escape lock of a
submarine.

Then the sirens would sound again and the nearby houses
would echo to the sound of refined and disciplined outrage
from their residents: "Mother, you've forgotten to pack the
sandwiches in the gas mask cases." "This is all getting to be
a nuisance; the Germans should think black shame of
themselves," and "Look, the shelter's flooded again."

So it was. The clear spring water coursing strongly under
the street and which gave rise to so many houses sagging at

their foundations had bubbled into the shelter once more, making the residents pause and reflect that they had two alternatives in that time of peril. They could either return to their homes and risk being blown into fragments or plunge into the shelter, which was now giving an imitation of a well-filled swimming pool, and bob about doing an agonised breast stroke or moody trudgeon crawl until the "all clear" sounded.

Viewing the vestigial remains of Wild Woodbine and Black Cat cigarette packets floating on the surface of the water, what seemed like the skeletal fragment of the wing of a strange tea-rose-pink bird or a piece of discarded corset and other objects, hard to define, that rose to the surface and sank in a curious and purposeless rhythm, the shelterers to a man, woman, child and household pet chose to return to their homes and hoped that the objects shed by the deciduous bombers would bounce off tenemental brick or sandstone walls of the sturdy urban keeps and explode harmlessly and without causing too much alarm to the lieges.

Edinburgh citizens had, for the most part, a not-too-dangerous war. German bombers on their way to the Clyde or other important targets might occasionally let slip an explosive device to annoy or amuse the inhabitants or jolt them out of their righteous sleep but generally they flew over the city, ignoring the noisy, vigorous but, it seemed to hyper-critical onlookers, not entirely accurate anti-aircraft defences.

Because of the unsuitability of our shelter, our family and most of our neighbours used to stand at their windows during an air raid and watch the passing show with the same absorbed interest of people observing a thunderstorm

Stuart MacGregor.

or watching a diver plunge 250 feet into a four-feet-high tank filled with blazing petrol.

The authorities, sensing the spectatorial tendencies of the British under fire, warned the populace not to do such foolhardy things in the event of a raid but to dash immediately for shelter. Since they did not realise that at least one batch of residents would need life-belts or even rubber dinghies and perhaps flares to survive a night in the cruel sea of our hideaway, we decided that if we could not flee or float we would enjoy the spectacle.

Looking back through the slit trench and civilian gas mask of memory, I realise that in the shelter of one of the city's tenements, built like a cross between a Border keep and a spur of Edinburgh Castle and which would probably have survived direct hits by a battery of howitzers, we saw a fairly regular programme that made today's television seem like puerile, watered-milk stuff.

Up there, under the glinting northern constellations, now apparently under the Plough, anon swerving towards Orion and then darting to some other star cluster, would be a German bomber caught in the multi-scissors' beams of searchlights. Tracer bullets stitched the dusky air, orange and yellow shell bursts patterned the skies and eventually all died away as the devilishly-cunning German made his passage across the North Sea, plentifully peppered, we hoped, by bits of good old British metal.

Later, we were all allocated another shelter where we sat with the residents of other houses, staring moodily at each other and some, myself included, wishing we were back in our observation posts watching the northern lethal lights of old Edinburgh making the Huns shiver in their flying jackboots and wish they had not grappled with the British bulldog breed.

Though I never met any, I was told at the time that some Edinburgh residents, cautious to the last, would go into their shelters wearing their gas masks and sit inhaling and exhaling heavily until the sirens sounded that the raid was over. Then they would emerge pink-faced and gasping like gaffed salmon and getting no fun out of the war at all.

We would have scorned such poltroonery in our building and some of us were only too anxious to get back—as we did when the war was well warmed-up and we were winning—to our houses to view what we gave to presumptuous Germans who invaded our air space that was redolent of soot, beer, dried eggs and military vehicle petrol fumes.

On a couple of occasions the Germans dropped bombs on the city, one so near us that the shock caused the water in our shelter to lap in a disturbed way; there was no depths to which the enemy would not sink. Mostly, however, they were characters in the occasional night spectacular and generally we appreciated the startling nature of the production.

The chances of window spectating in any future war, especially if it is nuclear, are, I suppose, slight. I have no doubt that the event would be spectacular though, possibly the most awesome show on earth. A pity not too many would be around to appreciate it.

19

Points of no return

A HOTEL once dubbed "Colditz" appears again in a new edition of the travel agents' "under the counter" guide to holiday hotels. Non-recommended hotels in the 1985 guide, published by Hogg Robinson Travel, include the Villa Rose complex at St George's Bay, Malta.

Last year the guide described it as looking like Colditz. This year it says: "A French tour operator uses it. Consequently there are now multinational escape committee meetings."

Previous criticisms of the Hotel Titanic in Benidorm with its "awful orange and purple" decor, which led to the BBC dispatching TV reporters to Spain to find out if it was as bad as the guide made out, has now been repainted cream "which includes painting the windows which many people would prefer to look through."

The Hotel Atlantida in Lloret, Spain, is described as "reminiscent of a cats' home with stray cats sleeping in the basement and all around the hotel." The hotel Ionian in Corfu is, according to the guide, like "a poor seamen's mission."

Dusty Miller, ex Flight 3127C from Gatwick, travel-hardened, wallet-ravaged air-borne veteran of Loophole Tours, stared bleakly at the scene before him—postcard-blue sea, golden sand that Beau Geste could have fought on with an Englishman's grace and hauteur, evocative signs on promenade cafe fronts like "Beer 'n Bite," "Tea like grandfather made" and John McStraps famous Stag's Breath Whisky," and rival gangs fighting it out on the beaches and thought wistfully of home.

It seemed like an age, although it was only three days since the heavy Spanish oaken doors creaked shut behind him as he checked in at the desk of the Hotel Torquemada ("breath-taking views of the new shopping complex, within easy reach of the airport and a stone's throw from the beach") and delivered himself up to the grim-faced male receptionist behind it who looked like a malevolent prune and talked in a way that suggested a heavy-weight flamenco dancer stamping his shoes on glass.

In the darkened diningroom, lit by one partially-guttering candle, the hotel's flimsy electric circuitry having been sabotaged earlier in an abortive attempt by some blundering Teutons to break free, Dusty looked at his fellow inmates and shuddered despite the heat, the glare and five glasses of eight star local brandy inside him that tasted like distilled saddle soap mixed up with sulphur, and which some said was made with boiled-down suitcases hastily left by travellers who had seen a chance to "make the break" and had taken it.

It was not an inspiring scene. Dejection was everywhere, the once proud spirit of the British holidaymaker that had brought fear and an embattled respect to many a foreign hotel, seemed to have disappeared like duty-free whisky down an honest British throat.

There was Snowy White, just out of Scunthorpe on his first continental holiday with his wife, an innocent chit of a slip of a girl who had broken down when she saw their room. No. 512, in the annexe, her "punishment cell" as she called it, with its picturesque peeling wallpaper, crushed beetle stains on the wall, inoperative telephones, jammed windows, sagging bed and hardly enough room to swing a tour courier or hotel proprietor.

Her screams on the first night were soul-rending. Dusty shook his head in the air that was heavy with sinister Spanish efforts to cook bacon and eggs the British way and tinned tomato soup that in colour was like a bad day in the bull ring and which tasted like a thrust from a banderillo.

The acrid reek of potato crisps that low-spirited inmates were getting high on in an effort to stave off the pangs of hunger was everywhere. This was no place for women or children, men either for that matter.

Even Mr J. and Mrs K. Trotter, ex-flight 2192A (Luton and Manchester) who had been everywhere, including there and back, who had been mugged in Majorca, left stranded by a failed holiday operator in Upper Volta, had their luggage lost at Malaga airport and escaped by the plaque on their false teeth when their hotel collapsed in another dented part of the Mediterranean basin, were gloomy.

"Easy reach of the airport, I'll say," muttered old man Trotter, his teeth grimly clenched after attempting to eat a Gibraltar-hard roll and a croissant that tasted on the tongue like garden gravel. "We're right against the main flight path. It's like being in Berlin during the airlift. Never had a wink of sleep at night for ten days. The beach? His eyes that were ringed with dark shadows from eating too many curdled gazpachos, lit up with a strange feverish light. "It's a stone's throw right enough, down a 500 feet sheer cliff."

Mrs Trotter buried her face in her handkerchief and wept, it was a face that only surfaced from behind the cloth during meal times to express displeasure at anything from broken bed springs to a collapsed souffle.

"Horror hotel ruined my dream holiday," she sniffled piteously, obviously preparing for the paid-for Press statement she hoped to make if ever she got back to the paradise of Mrs Thatcher's Britain.

Would she get back? Would any of them, who were stuck until the end of their holiday sentence in the huge concrete and glass structure that was shaped like a downmarket Aztec temple for ritual summer sacrifices.

Certainly some people had tried; brave spirits who had begged and pleaded with hard-faced holiday couriers to let them, because of their good behaviour and with no previous convictions for escaping their holiday ordeals, get home a week, say even a couple of days early. Some even suggested a swap with Spanish holidaymakers in Britain who might be suffering in British hotels, although that was hardly likely.

Their pleas were in vain. No flights were available, they were told, and even if they were, there was no guarantee that seats could be found for spineless dissidents. "Go and enjoy your holiday," they were told sternly, "like everyone else." Broken, dispirited, the holidaymakers went back to the hotel, their way flecked by muggers, battling Britons and Spanish policemen with striking good looks and matching accessories such as truncheons and revolvers.

"Ah you aff kom back," the sneering head waiter grinned with ill-suppressed satisfaction. "For you, it is the cannon-ball paella of such a weight that it will root you to the spot," he said, and, amid the groans of the tortured, strode off to welcome new arrivals to the diningroom.

There they were, fresh-faced and eager, straight from the training holiday camps, officers' mess type hostels and other ranks' boarding houses of Britain, captured by the

encircling movements of brochures and all unsuspecting of
the holiday hell that awaited them behind the concrete walls
and in front of the typical London-type bars.

Dusty Millar crumpled an unsmoked fag in his hand. His
face that had saddened at the sight, suddenly brightened.
He had only seven more days to go. Straightening up he
whistled a few bars of "Rule Britannia" and went in
unflinchingly to the gastronomic Gehenna that was the
diningroom at peak eating period. A Briton enduring a
holiday is a brave sight. Colditz never saw a braver.

20

Moles in my midst

SOMETIMES, when I am in a mood to pace the policies of this column, I venture into the rugged border areas and through powerful field-glasses, survey the adjoining territories.

I used to wonder whether there was life beyond this space but a careful analysis of what I have seen and heard convinces me that intelligences pulsate strongly on other parts of this page.

To the north there are the debateable lands of the letters, populated by often turbulent people, some good some bad, some perhaps, though I can hardly believe it, looking and behaving just like myself.

Beside them, to the east, is the delectable land of social events that seems to suggest, to me at any rate, a small Indian state of gilded palaces, aristocratic manors and spacious parklands, populated by the fair and the brave. To the west and north-west I can see the disputatious territories of the leading articles from which pronunciamentos toll with the slow, rhythmic, empasis of church bells.

To the south, I have discovered—though I search the area often with telescopes and radar scans—only what seems to be interminable space and sometimes when I have clambered on to some rugged, precipitous paragraph and looked out, I have suffered feelings of acute vertigo as if I could easily tumble into a gaseous nothingness, perhaps broken only be verbal asteroids, the slow spatial drift of meanings and the comet-like passing of fiery comments.

At the frontier areas, this column has, for security reasons, set up control posts, maintained by alert detachments of the area's own picked regiment, the 1st battalion, the Border Leicesters.

These posts teem with a life that to the eye of the stranger would suggest a prosperous and noisy bazaar in some of the more gregarious middle eastern countries.

Hawkers selling cut-price verbs, de-activated skilfully by a cunning that has been handed down through the centuries, stalls offering boxes of double-strength adjectives still wrapped in the original Cellophane and certain gentlemen willing to deliver lapidary phrases that are alleged to have fallen off the back of a columnar railway truck, no receipts, no cheques and only ready cash taken, can be seen in the milling throng.

From time to time, the guards initiate a random search among those crossing the frontier barriers to combat the illegal trade in untreated oxymoron and adulterated litotes that is unfortunately growing, but generally there is a free passage of the products of the areas—assertions, dogmatic statements, informed comment and occasionally, I am told, unfounded allegations.

To walk through any of these posts is to feel that one is standing at the crossroads of the world. Here we will see some word merchant struggling amid the hard laughter of spectators to put the cart before the horse, the air will be thick with the clamorous voices of those begging questions, little lads will be offering haughty strangers a quick "polish and parse" of any of their sentences and through it all will stride the columnar police, well known for their humorous indulgence to the quirks and foibles of humanity, but carrying, to show their authority, highly-polished and ready-for-action lethal questions that are carefully loaded.

Oh yes, I have strolled down the busy streets and alleyways, watching craftsmen replicate sentences of inordinate length and complexity that could not be distinguished from those used in this column, heard the merry laughter from hostelries as ideas were being lavishly entertained, and politely refused the blandishments of sloe-eyed, quick-moving, maidens offering me strangely scented grammar books, curious volumes on English usage or an interlude with any spicy sentence of my choice.

Unfortunately, the continual flow of movement across the frontiers brings its own problems. From time to time undesirable elements have been known to drift in—from where, who can say?—and get themselves appointed to positions of prominence in this column.

It is therefore with a great understanding of the position of British Leyland which unmasked 13 alleged Trotskyist "moles" at their Cowley motor manufacturing plant, that I can reveal that from time to time this column has been so riddled with such subversives that it resembled a nice bit of Gorgonzola cheese ready to take the biscuit.

Often these moles get themselves placed in strategic posts in this column so that they can learn its syntactical secrets which, in a cunning and ingenious microdotal manner, they transmit to rival concerns. Sometimes, they have broken into the columnar verbiage reserves and made off with vast raw crude supplies but generally their tasks seem to be to influence subtly the policies of this column from that of an extreme centrist organ of opinion to that of the far right or left.

Once, I discovered that a paragraph had been tampered

with so that it indicated that I fully supported the
expansionist policies of Genghis Khan.

"Who has committed this wretched and cowardly act?" I
thundered to the staff assembled in the gents' rest and video
room. There was a stunned silence which lasted but for a
few moments. Then, a temporary fused participle repairer,
who it turned out on careful examination, had been a
lecturer in political science but had fallen into dubious Left-
wing ways, stood up, brokenly confessed to the deed and
asked for 22 offences of deliberate typographical misspelling and malicious infinitive-splitting to be taken into
consideration.

I dismissed the man, who in his defence claimed that his
mind had been warped by his parents rearing him too early
on the works of Proudon and Bakunin, and told him never
to darken the sentence structure of this column again. He
left amid a solidarity of hisses from the staff.

Recently, as a result of information received, a detachment
of columnar police uncovered a batch of moles on the
sentence assembly line who spent much of their time
reading Left-wing propaganda to the honest artisans as
they worked at honing-down paragraphs or re-boring
phrases. Some of the workers claimed they were becoming
upset at being continually subjected to paragraphs from the
Morning Star and free translations from *Izvestia*.

When questioned, the moles admitted that they had been
placed in the column to turn it into an adjunct of *Pravada*
although somewhat more serious in intent than that, some
would say, flippant Soviet organ. Their voices, it was
noticed, were slurred and their breath smelled strongly of
the boiled-down pages of *Das Kapital*.

In matters of such delicacy I thought the woman's touch

would be appropriate. I asked Miss Angela Primstone, chatelaine of the columnar wine cupboard, to deal with the matter.

"Get out of here you wretched Marxist ruffians," she shrilled, and out they went, heads bowed and eyes, I suspected, misting with repentant tears.

That is the only way to deal with them. British Leyland and other companies, please take note.

21

Comma throes

LET me bring to readers' attention one Aldus Manutius, who, in case he is not already known to them, was born in 1450 in the Papal States, became a well-known publisher and in his Interpungedi Ratio, which appeared in 1466, wrote the following:

"That learned men are well known to disagree on this subject of punctuation is in itself a proof, that the knowledge of it, in theory and practice, is one of some importance. I, myself, have learned by experience that, if ideas that are difficult to understand are properly separated, they become clearer, and that, on the other hand, through defective punctuation many passages are confused and distorted to such a degree that they can with difficulty be understood, or even cannot be understood at all."

Well, if somewhat tortuously, said and while I and many others may find the learned Aldus's punctuation somewhat medieval, I am certain that we and whoever was responsible for composing an order from British Rail to preserve the elegant railway station at Drem, near Haddington,—a listed building—would agree with his general drift.

Because of a missing comma in the order, workmen began demolishing the waiting room and had stripped it of its rare fittings, windows, lavatories and roof before the error was discovered.

East Lothian District Council, rightly jealous of what railway heritage it has left, are insisting on the station being put back to the state it was before the squads got to work on it, including the restoration of a nineteenth century drinking fountain and cast-iron fittings.

While the order was for the station and nearby bridge to be preserved the crucial sentence read: "Drem station bridge should be retained . . ." instead of "Drem station, bridge, . . ." Because of the missing comma, the dismantlers though that only the bridge should be kept and that nearly all else was to be demolished.

In most cases, readers have a general idea of what a writer, despite any punctuation flaws, is getting at. A mistaken conclusion nevertheless could be reached that could cause nuclear-tipped missiles to wing their way across continents, a catastrophe that might have been readily avoided if the offenders had faced up to their grammatical responsibilities and had for instance, read *Modern English Usage* by Mr H.W. Fowler, the *Complete Plain Words* by Sir Ernest Gowers or their Russian or Chinese equivalents.

Readers who follow this column with the attention it may well deserve, will realise that I sprinkle it liberally with commas and similar high-quality and often expensive grammatical ingredients to bring out the subtle flavour of the words and improve the colour and texture of the sentences.

I am never without a packet of freshly-picked, newly-peeled punctuation marks to drop onto the page as I stir the subject up and bring it to the boil and I recommend their use to all eager aspirants in the craft of journalistic *haute cuisine*.

As the helmsman of an international organ of informed opinion, I realise that high-flown causes could sag like punctured hot-air balloons as a result of some technical fault in a sentence, shares could rise, business fall and deep inter-personal misunderstandings flare like Verey lights. It is a heavy and continuing responsibility.

When the full story of the British Empire comes to be written. I expect that the curious affair of the missing comma, the Ethiopian high command and myself, a small put perfectly formed corporal in the British Army, will be revealed.

In a privileged preview to the public I can say that apart from my military duties when fearlessly stationed in British Somaliland, I often gave advice to pencil-writing, lead-licking officers and other ranks on the finer points of English composition. "Corporal Morris," I would be told in the imperative mood, "the colonel wants advice on how to do a bit of *anterior* decoration for his regimental orders. Left right, left right, smartly now."

Up I would rush, even when not always in the indicative mood, my .300 all-weather, quick-loading, recoil-less pen at the port and my tense at the present. I would help the old warrior with his difficulties and take his campaign-scarred mind off the sun, sand, flies and fleas by showing him the various changes undergone by a verb—any verb—in order to show its voice, mood, tense and concord.

It was a conjugation devoutly to be wished because as a reward he sometimes let me escape from Somaliland as the NCO in charge of a three-ton lorry called the Kudu bus, after a species of buck, that delivered mail, civilians, Army personnel and goods between Somaliland's capital Hargeisa and Diredawa in Ethiopia.

One day on grammatical duty beside the native auxiliary verb camp, I was ordered to be in charge of the bus and told that my orders, syntactically perfect in all respects, would be handed to me by Giuseppe, an Italian driver and ex-prisoner of war with a formidable mouth of gold teeth and a superb bass baritone voice.

As we left the arid scrubland of the Somalis and entered the then lush landscape of Ethiopia, Giuseppe sang Italian opera selections in perfect continuous delivery. *La Traviata* came easily to his lips, so did *Il Trovatore* and by the time we got to our first halt, at Harar, to pick up mail and members of the Ethiopian high command, who were to go on manoeuvres in the interior, I was getting snatches of *Cavalleria Rusticana* and *L'Italiana in Algeri* bellowed in my flinching ear.

We stopped at the post office to collect letters. "We must now go to the barracks to pick up the officers," I said with a finger at the present indicative. "This is the barracks," bellowed Giuseppe as if he were Scarpia attempting to subdue Tosca. "See, it says in the orders: 'Post Office Armaresa Barracks.' There is mail but there are no officers. Andiamo. Let us go. Got to meet a nice friend at Diredawa."

Reluctantly, I agreed and on we sped through the smiling land of rich pastures and Ethiopians, at that time, all apparently glossy with good living.

"For me the war is over," shouted my driver as he manhandled the lorry wheel as if closing the doors of a giant dam. To celebrate that he sang the "Brindisi" from *La Traviata* which put me in a very tense mood.

On returning to Somaliland we were met at the frontier by a military police detachment. "Corporal Morris?" asked an NCO tersely. I nodded. As the Army expert in the subjunctive mood I could hardly deny it. "You are under arrest for not stopping at the Armaresa barracks and picking up the Emperor of Ethiopia's officers."

On the way back under escort Giuseppe pointedly hummed the "Miserere" from *Il Travatore* and I had the feeling that the fellow, knowing the true interpretation of the orders, had betrayed me like a common operatic villain.

It could have been a court martial for me but I was merely put on a charge. I appeared before the colonel who could have passed a severe sentence on me if he could have constructed one.

Asked what I had to say I pointed out that the orders had no commas between the words post office and barracks. I assumed that the post office was in the barracks.

The colonel glared at the orders and harrumphed: "Quite right. A missing comma could have sent you to jail for a period. Charge dismissed."

"Thank you sir," I said and saluted. Thank you Aldus; I salute you as well.

22

Not just a news story

ONE of the hazards of a journalist's life—especially that of reporters engaged in the daily gathering of news events, ranging say from sickening carnage in Beirut to noting the results at some Scottish Women's Rural Institute jam-making and soft-toy competition—is that a certain insensitivity to the convulsions of the human spirit tends to appear in the most compassionate of writers.

A reporter covering his first fatal accident story might be shocked at a thunderbolt flung by malevolent fate into some section of mankind and the effect it had on kith, kin and community but after opening his notebook on say, the tenth such assignment, the first, keen horror might tend to become somewhat blunted.

Thus, a newsman mixing with kings, conmen, sinners and those who could pass for saints, and using his busy pencil and pad to record the aspirations, failures, triumphs, disasters and the curious, menacing and endearing behaviour of mankind, tends to develop a kind of carapace that isolates him from sharing too fully in the grief or exultation of some news event.

It must, I think, be so. Too close involvement could prevent him or her from the efficient collection of facts and transforming them into impactive news stories or feature articles, thus endangering the flow of copy to the presses and resulting in the ire of sub-editors, ever hungry for the unimpeded supply of news.

In my own career I must have written a trackless desert of print concerning stories about the fate of cycling malcontents found at night without lights (fined £1), murder, mayhem, chicanery at national and local government level, pious hopes, impious deeds, and other newsworthy tales showing man at his inspirational best and bestial worst.

For the most part they belong to a great, jumbled, kaleidoscope of headlined memory through which, at imperative recall, gesticulating politicians, bellowing street demonstrators, judges delivering death sentences, juries giving "not guilty" verdicts, lawyers arguing their cases with the verbal equivalent of cutlasses or rapiers while the murder-accused sat puppet-like and apparently uncaring in dock, and the faces of families moved to sudden joy or tears, appear and then vanish, giving no indication of the adjectival or verbal strain involving in reporting the stories aright.

Any emotion I may have had during my contact with such events was necessarily muffled by the technical effort of having to write about them. Thus, I suppose, a surgeon must feel, as he sees yet another patient wheeled into him for physical amendment. Whatever pity he might have for the still, fragment of humanity under him, attached temporarily to the theatre's life support system, it must be suspended and cool, professional judgment and manual dexterity substituted so that the task can be performed as successfully as the latest surgical methods will allow.

Continual experience dulls the emotions and so the great reading and viewing public, untouched personally as yet by joyful or horrific events around them, tend to become anaesthetised by daily exposure to newspaper-reported events or those seen through the cold, dispassionate eyes, of TV cameras.

A Vietnamese child, hideously burned by the obscenity of napalm, the patient, large-eyed, famine-stricken masses of Africa resembling elongated stick insects, the sight of a teenage Argentine soldier near to tears at Mass in Port Stanley while waiting for the British to close in, and the wounded and charred dead from the bombed ships in San Carlos Bay, have the power to move us temporarily, but no doubt there is always something on another channel to take our minds off the more soul-piercing realities of life on this tortured planet.

Such events, alas, become just mere news stories, to be read about or viewed for a time, then buried mercifully in the lumber room of memories that are perhaps best forgotten since they make us aware of the fragile threads on which our lives dangle.

Certain events do stand out in my newspaper memories, etched with a clarity that the years cannot dim. One concerned an assignment I had as a young reporter to interview a Musselburgh mother who lived in Goose Green, a name now hauntingly linked with the South Atlantic, whose son, reported missing during the fighting in Korea, had just been found safe and well.

For some reason, I arrived before the official War Office telegram. The woman, a housewife in her fifties with the kind of wrinkled, lived-in face that some women get from an adulthood of housework, family cares, raw climate and living in the bracing austerities of Scotland, seemed momentarily stunned.

Then her face lit up in a sunburst of a smile, the recollection of which warms me yet and she flung her arms about me and wept. Our photographer, sensing that a picture was worth 1,000 words—1,000 of mine at any rate—took a shot of the scene. I have it yet, the bringer of good news is, I have always felt, peculiarly favoured by fortune.

Another event that I can never erase even from my furtive memory was being sent, as an office junior to collect a photograph of a young Royal Air Force officer killed during the last war.

I made my way to a house in one of Edinburgh's quiet suburbs, pointed out my errand and was shocked when the man's mother called me into her still, dark, house, handed me the photograph and burst into hot, fierce, tears.

Her cries echoing in the cold, dark rooms, the portrait of the smiling young man, trim and jaunty in his officer's uniform, affected me greatly. "Listen laddie," said the woman, trying to raise the pitful ghost of an apologetic smile. "Don't mind about me. Take the photograph. I know it's just your job."

The outer journalistic skin cracks and crumbles leaving the emotional vulnerabilities exposed when a story occurs in which one has become involved beyond that of the demands of the job.

Thus, I and all my colleagues who worked with her when she was a journalist on *The Scotsman* some years ago, extend to Mrs Liz Maxwell of Cramond Hill Farm, Cornhill-on-Tweed, Northumberland, and her husband Fordyce, a former agricultural editor on this paper, our feelings of shock and horror at the news of their daughter Susie being found foully murdered; an outrage that has, I think, shocked and haunted all Britain.

Perhaps readers might like to know that Liz occasionally brought little Susie into the office and introduced her to the staff who were always ready to lay down a news item for a moment and have a chat with the pretty, cheerful, child.

Now, that little fragment of happy innocence has been crushed out of existence by a thunderbolt from fate and we are left with a deep sorrow, a profound rage and a terrible impotence.

Not just another news story for us. Not now. Not ever.

23

Feet in the sky

YOU may not think it to look at me but I can remember the German airship Graf Zeppelin which flew over Edinburgh one day of light cloud when the city was not thinking of anything in particular and was humdrumming away on its normal routine of being the northern metropolis and, as Robert Louis Stevenson succinctly put it "a meteorological purgatory."

I was either engaged on some now-forgotten childhood activity or brooding on the nature of the universe when my mother rushed into my room in a whirl of excitement and informed me that an air-ship was immediately overhead and that if we moved into another room at a brisk trot we might be in time to see it.

As we did so, I was immediately aware of a sound resembling about 100 clockwork toy car engines operating in unison but when I peered into the grey sky of that otherwise undistinguished day in the 1930s, I saw no gleaming, cigar-shaped, lighter-than-air pride of the Teutons but a vague shape that I took to be the last of the craft's stern disappearing into a glowering Scottish cloud that was about as thick and colourful as prison gruel.

My disappointment, though acute for a few seconds, was accepted with childhood stoicism. I have since met other people of my own age who saw the ethereal vision on that day and many told me they were transfixed with pleasure and held up their little pink, grubby Midlothian hands in an attitude of wonder.

Some said that the sight opened up magic casements for them into faery lands of technical speculation and made them hope that one day they would fly in such craft themselves to far-off countries and that eventually every industrious and deserving Scottish family would have a small Zeppelin in the garage to take them to work, on holiday or on weekend flights to respectable hotels for lunch or afternoon tea.

At that time, the skies above Edinburgh, apart from city and migratory birds, were fairly empty. Occasionally a rickety biplane of wood and wire or monoplane fashioned in early attempts at streamlining, would drone over the city and sometimes one would suddenly indulge in a series of aerobatics trailing coloured smoke from the tail. This would be shakily transformed into a series of letters which formed some lofty and compelling sentence like: "Buy Persil."

The city would temporarily clatter, stumble and screech to a halt while the crowds gazed at this sign from the skies. People would then mutter, probably in superstitious awe then go about their business shaking their scandalised heads at the desecration of the noble air with gross commercialism and either forget the product that was advertised or crossly resolve—such is the contra-suggestible nature of the city—not to buy it.

Regret for missing the airship, though stifled in me with semi-stiff upper lip, did not entirely disappear. I used to dream that a Zeppelin, a creation of silver and gold would appear in the sky as in some divine visitation and which would seem to be the sudden harbinger of delight for me. Tramcars in my dreams were also symbols of happiness and a Zeppelin overflying a city tramcar—preferably a No. 6 Marchmont Circle one—could have me yelling in my

Stewart Macgregor.

sleep for sheer joy and putting the rest of the family in a state of acute irritation.

I have always regretted that the Zeppelin was somehow foredoomed in the development of aircraft from the hot air balloonistics of the Brothers Montgolfier to the latest space shuttle craft.

It seemed to be a line as fated for extinction as Neanderthal man or the great reptiles and yet the craft had grace, and a certain, slow-moving and deliberate efficiency like a great semi-somnolent fish.

I can remember seeing films of passengers embarking on the German airships that were proclaimed as the last word in comfortable air travel and were symbols of the nation's ingenuity, construction skill and technical and industrial resurgence after its defeat in the First World War.

There they were, the grinning members of the hydrogen set, the men dressed in smart double-breasted suits, with hair well slicked back and madny having the cheerful boyishness and occasional upper-class vacancy that often appeared on the features of the late Duke of Windsor when he was Prince of Wales. The women wore classic suits, had hair that was a sea of Marcelle waves and the crew were either dressed in smart steward suits or had uniforms that had a distinctly nautical touch. The captain—you could never call him the pilot—was in gear that resembled that of a U-boat commander about to receive the Iron Cross first class from the Kaiser.

Teutonic taste and the dictates of power-weight ratios resulted in a variety of wicker-work furniture being placed in these craft. There were, I recall, lace curtains and aspidistras and the general atmosphere seemed that of a well-appointed hotel in a good-class district of Berlin.

There was also, if memory does not betray me, a small ballroom in which couples danced, with, as it were, their feet on the clouds, to the music of a small but well-disciplined string orchestra.

Ah, what a glamour, what thrill to be aloft, incumbent on the respectful air, droning over the mountains, rivers, nations, principalities of Europe that would soon see grim and lethal craft massing in the sky and in that voyage of comfort and elegance what frisson of excitement to experience when someone highly prominent in Burke's Peerage or the Almanach de Gotha might sniff disdainfully and ask: "Anyone smell burning?"

The airship was also the scene of international spy thrillers and at least one film where the sinister central European agent with plans of the new British interceptor triplane was matched against the young, cricket-loving Englishman drawn into the espionage game inadvertently.

Not only Germany but America, Britain and Russia are taking a new interest in airships, lifted by helium instead of hydrogen but also powered by nuclear reactors, driven by turbofans, one—incredibly—by swivel-mounted helicopters on crossbeams, and another—an American conception—driven by self-propelled radial wings.

In Britain, John West Associates, of London, plan to build prototype airships shaped like flying saucers, and Thermo Skyships, of the Isle of Man, are trying to attract money to build such craft.

One day—I can see it now—I will be sitting in a tramcar in that reintroduced transport system in Edinburgh and not thinking much about anything when someone will nudge me in the ribs and say: "Look, an airship!" and up there, shaped like a large torpedo, glinting silver in the sullen northern sky, will be the Zeppelin of my dreams and my childhood regret will vanish in adult wonder. What joy! I can hardly wait for such uplift.

24

Scenes from my life

FOR the first time in many months I went to a cinema the other night. It was a dismal experience and one I do not intend to repeat for a long time, if ever.

Apart from the main film, in my valuable opinion a tedious and over-acted production, the three-and-a-half-hour period of my attendance at that pagoda of alleged pleasure was taken up with a small travel film of extraordinary dullness of script and cliche-filled scenes, advertisements, a trailer and an inordinately-long period of background taped music during which white-overalled female acolytes bearing trays dispensed ice cream and assorted metallic-tasting fruit juices.

For that encounter in a theatre which had the area underneath the seats almost ankle-deep in the detritus of the throwaway society, I paid £4.60 for two tickets, money which in this case I grudge when I compare it with the relatively low price of cinema tickets in my youth and early manhood and the often excellent value one received in what may well have been the golden age of the cinema.

I am well aware that the steep rises in film production and cinema maintenance costs, staff wages and the price of projection equipment must inevitably lead to high admittance charges and these I would not mind paying if only we got anything like the rich variety of entertainment in this cinema that used to be offered.

Nowadays, although we are seated in the latest sub-divided, box-like structures with projection equipment of an

121

excellence undreamed of in the days when I was but a young film-staring lad, I do not leave cinemas with the same sense of having been superbly entertained as I did at one time. Intervals between films now seem to be longer and stretching out every year, second films seem to be shorter—if we get any at all—and advertisements serve only to take our minds temporarily off the money we have paid at the box-office and sweet counter.

I see from a newspaper report that a 1920s cinema of the type once affectionately known as the "flea pit" has been rebuilt inside the new Leeds Industrial Museum which opened the other day.

The cinema, big enough to seat a school class, will show on its 1924 Leeds-made projectors clips of films shot in the city at the turn of the century, cowboy adventures of the 1940s and educational films.

While I applaud the enterprise of the city council in including such an example of folk art and entertainment in their museum, I should be surprised if the authentic atmosphere of these ancient enclaves, dedicated to helping the masses forget for a while the rent, rates and the rain, the soot-begrimed factories and commercial buildings, the Lowry-type houses, people and dogs that made up the environment of so many of our cities and towns in the twenties and thirties, can be accurately recreated.

What cinema, in the essentially sterile atmosphere of a museum, can evoke the peculiar setting and scent of these old picturehouses. What municipal illusionist—even on a temporary basis—can bring back the feeling that, as one entered some of the architecturally-exotic cinemas, we were stepping into some doge's palace, some rich hidalgo's castle in castanet-clicking, gypsy-skirt-swirling, flamenco-singing Spain or even into the seraglio's quarter of some fabled sultan of the gorgeous East?

Ah, how the old names come back to one like the tolling of a bell at the great gate of Kiev in Mussorgsky's *Pictures at an Exhibition*—the Alhambra, the Majestic, the Palace, the Regal, the Regent and the Colosseum. Names to roll on the mind's tongue like a praline which when cracked would perhaps give off the genuine flavour and scent of each establishment.

In so many of these cinemas there was an odour that was made up of the combined scents of disinfectant, a heavy perfume laid down by the staff to combat, but which seldom did, the peculiar smell and miasma from wet raincoats, pixie hoods, umbrellas and cigarette smoke, the scent of sweets being crunched incessantly with the noise of distant small-arms' fire and above all that an unidentified scent, sweet, even sickly, but always in my mind associated with the cinema immediately before and for at least two decades after the Second World War.

In some cinemas the management maintained a hygienic ritual of cleaning and spraying that would not have looked out of place in a hospital ward. There always seemed on the premises some work-bent female eternally scrubbing stairs or vacuuming some expanse of threadbare carpet. Squads of sweepers were continually engaged in cleaning out spent ice-cream cartons, chocolate wrapping paper, ear-rings, gloves and odd shoes left by the patrons.

Some of the children's matinees were continually subjected to spraying with disinfectants by usherettes who viewed their audience with deep suspicion that they might have on their tiny persons the bacilli of diseases ranging from tick fever to rinderpest.

The grim-faced women would sweep up and down the aisles drenching the tots in spray like aeroplanes bombarding nomadic locusts. Such interludes caused a temporary halt in the normal hubbub of children's cinema and a cessation in the innumerable battles fought between children when the subject matter on the screen palled, as it did whenever anything like love interest reared its boring head.

You got saturation-entertainment in those days. A main feature film would be followed by a "B" movie, often of excellent visual and intellectual grip, sometimes a small documentary, always the newsreel and often with the gravel-voiced Leslie Mitchell reporting, a cartoon, sometimes two, the trailer, occasionally more than one, and only a few—if any—advertisements.

As a child I would often cling to my seat like chewing gum on a bedpost and see the full programme twice, coming out perhaps blinking in the late afternoon with a splitting headache and curious blue spots flashing before my eyes but satisfied that I had received my money's worth.

Some cinemas seemed to have a perpetual atmosphere of deep gloom and foreboding and it was fitting that these often showed horror films that specialised in vampires sliding out of their coffins when the moon was full in a sky of ragged cloud, or alien creatures of unrefined mien and even coarser appetites dropping in on some friendly, unsuspecting middle-West community.

Then there were the commissionaires, many-medalled and besashed men with the uniforms of Ruritanian rear-admirals who marshalled the queues with the precision of punctilio of Guards' RSMs on parade, quietening the 1s 9d rabble with a look and speaking reassuringly to the half-crowns and three shillings, telling them that there was every chance of a seat that night and would they please close up their ranks and not straggle so much.

How I remember the richness of carpets, the profusion of potted palms, the sensual drape of curtaining material and the manager himself, standing in all his evening-suited glory eyeing with sober satisfaction the crowds surging in, now with a regal nod allowing a couple of complementary ticket-holders to scuttle in gratefully, anon shaking his head regretfully to tell old and respected patrons that they might have to queue for another hour before he could let them in and later telling some errant couple in a voice of cold command that they had to join the patient ranks that snaked round adjoining buildings and could not just slip in as they liked.

All gone alas, like my youth and the days of the Kerry dancing too soon, the few remaining cinemas, sometimes ill-kept and tawdry, with grimy carpets and unswept floors and often showing films of—in my admittedly biased view—expensive banality.

Still, I remember the old places in the ever-open cinema of my memory. With today's seat prices in the real-life theatres I shall have to be content to give my mind's eye ever-increasing treats. It will soon be all I can afford.

25

The bitter cup

CIVIL servants are no longer to be allowed to brew tea in their offices, according to a newspaper report. Tea trolleys are to be replaced by automatic vending machines.

The Government, according to the story, are to take a fresh look at catering in the Civil Service following the Rayner report last month which criticised the appearance of offices cluttered with milk bottles and tea pots.

The decision has already been opposed because it will mean disbanding the office tea clubs which union leaders say are the basis of a wide range of Civil Service social activities.

A spokesman for the Civil and Public Services Association, the biggest Civil Service union, said that tea was part of the image of the service. "We have put up with the jibes over the years in good spirit ... A move like that could seriously damage morale."

Miss Penelope Griff, clerical officer and unofficial plenipotentiary for the purchase of tea, biscuits and buns in their season for her room, paused in her work of helping to amass statistics of white fish landings—off Rockall—and gazed at her colleagues with a sombre and reflective eye.

They worked in a typical scene of administrative industry that could be mirrored on thousands of similar rooms all over civil serviced Britain. Jackson, executive officer— don't ask her how he got that post, the man could hardly operate the memory banks of a basic pocket calculator without getting mind and thumb sprain—was hunched like a galley slave over his oar at his desk, a phone apparently growing our of his ear, taking down the latest Test match scores.

Miss Glowrie, clerical assistant and candidate for Scotland's most original speller title but a tea-maker of extraordinary, some said uncanny, powers, was also hard at it, taking down the day's quick recipe over the telephone—this time devilled gooseberries with sauerkraut—which busy housewives often reached for before the stomach pump and the urgent ambulance. Mr J.V. Numb, administrative trainee, was also at a task of essential civil servicing—the arranging of fixtures for the department's golf and skittle clubs—and indeed all were gainfully occupied, the sleeves of their minds rolled up as they calculated what their index-linked pensions would be worth when they laid down their official tea-cups for the last time, how many weeks it was to their next paid leave and what sort of work they could pick up when they left the service full of pensions, honours and farewell presents.

The scene, apart from the stern desks, austere files and unswerving statistics, the last cunningly designed by the highest brains of the service to prove anything to anyone at any time, was nevertheless homely.

Tea-cups, some full, some empty and some with a quantity of liquid that left a neat brown ring in their interiors, were dotted over desks, on window shelves, the floor, in cupboards and in filed boxes marked "L" for "liquid containers"—the last activity, the work of Miss E. Prittstock, clerical assistant extraordinary, her motto "I file 'em, you find 'em"—and some even spilled out into the corridors of moderate power where they mingled with the stock of other rooms.

Miss Griff knew that from the lowest messenger with the acne carriage and the stride of a gigantic stick insect to those godlike beings who sat in lofty, airless and thick-carpeted rooms in obscure parts of the building and who rejoiced soberly but persistently under the titles of principal, assistant secretary, deputy secretary and even—the dread words trembled on her mental lips—permanent secretary, all were sustained, comforted, and fuelled by endles supplies of tea.

There was nothing a civil servant, labouring heavily perhaps under the compilation of information about increased penalties for the slaughter regulations of natterjack toads or information about great white shark fishing in the Clyde, liked better than hearing a regulation supply of water being poured in the statutory time into a stock Civil Service kettle.

It was what the nightingale was to Keats, the mouse to Burns, the rainbow and the daffodil to Wordsworth, Gunga Din to a thirsty, bullet-nicked British soldier and a rosy-cheeked young maid to Count, as Bram Stoker had it, Dracula.

Miss Griff moistened her lips, that could tighten like a steel spring when she faced the latest challenging statistics' compilation on the incidence of wild cat flea fever among schoolchildren in council housing estates in North-west Scotland, and recalled wistfully the day when she was admitted to the service and told by a stern but just official, "You are entering a new world of dedication to duty, responsibility, hard work with often inadequate rewards, but whatever befalls you, there will always be all the files, paper clips, pens, glue guns and indiarubbers you can use and all the tea you can drink. Away with you and take your first cup."

So she did. To this day she remembered it, in a tannin-stained, chipped mug entitled "Charlie Fergusson his property." It was the colour of nutmeg but with the heat of ginger and it seemed to sing to her as it passed through her digestive system of happy, busy days telephoning for her sporting superiors the latest cricket scores and weather forecasts and maybe, yes maybe if she applied herself diligently, dialing time or even being asked to get for some higher-up colleague, about to go on holiday, a road report from the AA.

These were stirring times and she remembered how she herself made the supplies for her office, how the lads pinched her tea bags playfully and told her to "put another leaf in it," how she blushed when told by a senior executive officer that one day she herself would be worthy of a top job in the service with a pot of English breakfast and a top-quality macaroon all to herself.

Ah old days, old ways, Miss Griff dropped a tea-stained tear into the cup that had just arrived steaming along with a pile of unsweetened statistics about tooth-decay among black polled bullocks in Central Scotland.

Now, even if that top post did come and she could sip the invigorating taste of success, there would be no equivalent supply of Swatow Breakfast with its delicate and evocative scents of ancient bamboo, sun dried paddy fields and wet sails of junks on the Yangtse.

Word had already got round that the first of the Civil Service tea vending machines had arrived—a big brute with a look of hauteur on its dial like a principal approached by an underling for extra holiday leave—which dispensed with accuracy variations on a theme of hot liquidity that the masses gulped with a look on their faces that might indicate relish.

As the representative of the room commissariat, she approached the machine with a wary air. She had heard much about them, how they sometimes took money but gave nothing in return, how they gave coffee white instead of tea, black, without, and how sometimes they either dropped a carton tasting of soup (onion) coffee with, fruit drink (unsugared) and something that resembled axle grease or shot a jet of clear, hot water on to the hand upreached to take its paid-for cup of liquid.

She popped in her coins and the machine obliging dropped her a cup of coffee. Then, unexpectedly, another and another. All three tasted satisfactory and Miss Griff thrilled to think that at heart the machine was a civil servant and could work in triplicate.

As she sipped her coffee, looked on the real world outside and dialled a bed-time story that she could relate to the staff later, Miss Griff was moderately happy. A new leaf had been turned in the Civil Service; perhaps, only perhaps, mind you, it was not the bitter cup she imagined and all might be for the best in the best of all possible worlds.

26

Magic and Marx

THERE are times when I feel the world is too much with me and that getting and spending I not only lay waste my powers but also put too much steam into the economy.

It is then that I pick up books that gripped my mind in childhood and made me believe, even at an age when I was just over reading with my index finger and mouthing Mother Goose, that there might be in this planet a strong, unswerving, moral force that doled out rewards and punishments and that if I kept myself pure in thought, word and deed, like some of the characters I read about, and washed carefully behind the ears, I might become a prominent citizen secure in the knowledge that multitudes would smile when I smiled or tremble with fear at my frown.

These books, and I confess it freely, are known as fairy tales and they include other children's classics such as *Black Beauty, Robinson Crusoe* and *Gullivers' Travels*. In them, I am transported from a world of wars, rumours of wars, rents, rates and taxes, malevolent and beneficent bacteria and reeling with all the large and petty crimes and persistent follies of mankind, through magic casements into fairy lands distinctly unforlorn where every rainbow contains a pot of gold that, while it cannot be invested in Imperial Chemical Industries, can at least be used to good effect in happy-ever-after land to maintain an adequate standard of living.

You know where you are with fairy tales. They not only deal with the uncertainties of life, which readers know about only too well, but make it clear that virtue will be rewarded, evil punished, often in exquisite agony, and that the young will die good if they die at all.

The old will also get their rewards or deserts, depending on whether or not they eat children, blind princes or turn them deftly into bluebirds or are good fairies undergoing metamorphosis for a spell.

There is, for me, a distinctly durable quality about some of these tales especially by Hans Andersen or the aptly-named Brothers Grimm. They are like symbolic giants, gnarled, old oak trees with deep roots in a mental earth that is fertilised by race memories, primitive instincts and uncomplicated emotions. They possess their own form of magic that can transport minds, certainly children's minds, into rich realms of imagination and speculation and pure narrative delight. Besides them, the Enid Blytons and modern writers with similar tale-telling techniques seem, in my view, as pale, scentless and even sickly flowers.

The well-loved and often-told tales which can still draw even old men from the spittoon or the bookies and children from vandalising their grandmother's money box, have been for years psychological meat and drink for those who see in them Freudian, Jungian and Adlerian symbols which include sex, violence and perhaps even sibling rivalry and covert or overt Marxist economic theory as well as illustrations of the lumpen peasant classes being trodden on by the invariably better-looking rich.

On the basis that one could, if one wished, find Confucian philosophy in Mrs Beeton's recipes or the quintessence of British colonial policy in Africa in the stories of Little Black

Sambo, I am always interested in such intellectual gropings into our childhood literature.

The latest attempt to find the inner meanings of fairy stories is reported from the United States where over the last weekend, academics—psychiatrists, language experts, anthropologists, and sociologists—met at Princeton University to dissect, with finely-sharpened intellects, these tales that can still hold millions of children entranced at their mother's knee or father's elbow.

According to Professor Jack Zipes, of the German language department of the University of Wisconsin, a self-described Marxist, Little Red Riding Hood is "a narrative of rape in which the heroine is expected to bear the responsibility for sexual violation."

That interpretation certainly never occurred to me when I lisped it aloud in my story books up to the age of 17. I always thought it was a tale about age concern, transvestitism, aberrant lupine behaviour and the acute powers of observation and quick-thinking of little girls. It was as simple as that. I learned about women at an early age from such stories.

Professor Ruth Bottigheimer, organiser of the conference, who teaches literature and Germanic languages at Princeton—there's glory for you perhaps to exceed that of the Sultan Haroun Al Raschid sitting among his riches and listening to some Sheherazade telling tales of the seven scurvy sons of Sinbad—believes that there is a distinct anti-woman bias in many of the tales. "When a woman speaks, she is almost always defined as wicked," she says. "Thus, the first time Gretel tries to make herself heard, Hansel snaps: 'Be quiet, Gretel.'"

I dispute that assertion entirely. Women and girls emerge

in many of these tales as, if not heroines, at least characters with quick wits, sharp eyes and ready tongues who can run rings round their male counterparts. Even the female villains often possess a presence that seems a combination of the more formidable characteristics of Catherine the Great and the daughters of Count Dracula getting edgy after trying to exist on a vegetable diet.

I can fully understand the concern of Hansel for silence as he and his sister removed the pointing with their teeth from the house of gingerbread, a dwelling that could seriously damage the health in its concentration of carbohydrates. If the witch owner heard them they were likely to end up as the *plat du jour,* fricasseed or lightly fried in batter and with a side salad.

I admit that the life of a female in such tales was one of sudden rises and falls in fortune, like Australian copper shares. One minute a princess, the next tossed out of the palace by the wicked step-mother queen and made to tend swine or geese until the arrival of the handsome prince; one day kept in a tower for the express purpose of growing your hair to allow a witch entrance and egress by climbing or descending it and the next being woo'd by a handsome scion of the monarchy who is immediately blinded by the owner and only has his sight restored when his eyes are washed by the heroine's tears, the fluid obviously containing some powerful anti-biotic ingredient.

The greatest heroine of course is Alice who, with the prim and purposeful attitude of a Victorian governess or headmistress, puts the Wonderland characters firmly in their places, finally dismissing them with the scornful: "You're nothing but a pack of cards." Thus did we scatter the Queen Empress's foes and bring law and our idea of order to an empire.

It is possible that there are aspects of the class struggle in tales like Aladdin which could be subtitled "genie with the light brown heir," and an example of the redistribution of property in Ali Baba and the 40 Thieves, and I expect the girl who had to sit sewing, like sister Susie, shirts for her brothers who had been turned into swans, no doubt could be used as an example of Marx's theory of surplus value.

What impressed me as a child about fairy tales was that they let you know that all was not sweetness and light in the world. In it were treachery, mendacity, cupidity, sudden violence, instant and sometimes lingering death, but at the same time a world of goodness rewarded, badness thwarted and with a good fairy generally available—like an insurance claims official—who would not make a drama out of a catastrophe.

It may be that one will find illustrations of dialectic materialism, the alienation of the worker and even his depersonalisation, not to mention—but trust me to do so— the struggle between capital and labour in *The Water Babies,* Rumpelstiltskin and the Ugly Duckling but I prefer to read such tales only for their constant ability to enchant even the adult mind. Despite the gibberings of such academics, I shall be into *Alice Through the Looking Glass* soon—perhaps quicker that it takes one to get from here to Babylon and back by candlelight.

27

A shrike of parking anguish

KEEN observers of the wild and domestic life of Scotland's capital will, no doubt, be familiar with the many migrants that visit us annually and bring so much interest, intellectually and—what is better—financially, to its inhabitants.

There are, of course, thousands of birds of pay, or tourists, sometimes unkindly referred to as boobies or nuthatches, depending on how free they are with cash which, occasionally, is delivered through their noses—a quaint, charming and continually rewarding action. Their plumage is often a bright seersucker or travellers' check and they can be observed at hotel reception desks in ritual displays of departure, indulging in bill snapping and wild flapping.

At this time of the wildlife year, one can also spot what trained watchers know as the conference pair, usually an old bustard with his secretary bird taking part in the mass migratory meetings of similar species which gather in the larger halls, indulge in gin and bitterns, loud squawks and much protective mimicry.

Lately, however, there has been much informed talk of a visitor which has been in the city for some time but appears to be increasing in numbers now challenging even those of the city starlings.

This new species can be distinguished by its sombre plumage, brightended by a vivid yellow band around the head, eagle-eyes and a steady, measured tread and,

Stuart MacGregor.

although given to slow bipedal locomotion, it can dart off with startling swiftness when prey is sighted.

The male is larger, usually unadorned, shows a bold, authoritative sternum, and pads along with notebooks. The female often has a pouch or bag dangling parallel to the humerus, although you had better not let her catch you laughing, and some have dark-framed circles over their eyes, no doubt to prevent the sun from blinding them as they scan the area for the first sign of a fly character.

The species is known as the Common Warden or Tyrant Carcatcher. Its distribution is now apparently nation-wide, and it congregates in cities where the pickings are largest, multiplying at an alarming rate.

The newcomers are, in fact, one of the lower strata of a pecking order which works to feather the nest of the Large Dodo or Corporation Shear-robber which feeds ravenously on fine fare and makes the errant and erring Gulled Driver—and there are masses of them uttering their melancholy cries in the city—quail or shrike in parking anguish.

So grateful is the dominant predator for the action of the Common Warden that it has caused roosting areas to be included in its defended territory from which the warden can take off, known as parking meters or soar points.

While some see wardens as a tern for the worse, it has, in fairness, to be pointed out that many are very friendly but have a talon for spotting fresh, crisp and juicy untruths displayed by their prey. Try telling them that you have left your car at an illegal parking place because you ran out of petrol and you could find yourself hauled up before a municipal beak.

I keep seeing swarms of wardens in the city, now wheeling

left, now darting right as if about to migrate but, of course, they never do. A friend reported one winging her way home, no doubt after a hard day looking for motoring worms, humming what sounded suspiciously like: "You toucan be the life of the party."

I find that hard to swallow but I will.

28

Scrawl of the wild

SOMETIMES, when I look at the badly-spelled, banal and often inscrutable graffiti scrawled about the old grey capital of Scotland, I wonder whether this country is doing enough to support what has now become a traditional folk art and whether there is any danger of these free-lance artists disappearing from our streets, leaving only a pathetic bit of smudged paint to mark their passing.

Not long ago, in an obscure alleyway in a dismal and decrepit part of the city centre I saw a graffito that one day might be as rare as the prehistoric cave paintings of the Dordogne. By an unknown artist, executed on a background of decayed brick and peeling paint, its message was about as impactive to the senses as an El Greco: "There's more to life than meets the mind." It said in colours of rust-brown and acid green.

That work told me more about the state of Scotland and its artistic pretentions than a wilderness of Arts Council reports. Here was a flower born to blush unseen and waste its sweetness in anonymity; talent squandered, not to mention the time and money for the tin of spray paint.

I felt that while there was no shortage of mediocre practitioners of the art of instant art, if the last word is the *mot juste,* there were few—if any—of the old masters left to gladden the eyes of your ordinary humdrumming citizen who only wants a bit of colour in his or her drab life.

In any country worthy of its artistic asprations, that

work would have been preserved under special conditions with temperature and humidity just right and only a certain number of viewers allowed to visit it—say a couple of weeks in January only. Around it, National Gallery custodians would be selling postcards of the work and brochures about the history of graffiti and explaining the techniques involved.

England does these things better. I have before me a report that the art-loving London burgh of Camden recently invited Brim Fuentes, the so-called graffiti king of New York's subway system to London, armed with cans of paint, to take part in a two-week festival organised by that Left-wing and progressive body.

He was flown over at a cost of £800—a mere bagatelle in terms of ratepayers' money—to the Greater London Council, the Inner London Education Authority which, with the burgh, are funding the Festival.

When he arrived he laughingly reassured Londoners by saying: "I know people are scared I will encourage graffiti. Let them relax. The stuff I do can only happen in New York. I am only spraying on canvas in London.

Brim, aged 19 and as colourful a character as those he daubs on New York, especially around its railway system, has sold many of his "legitimate" canvasses for over £800 each.

The public appear to love him and the New York police would also like a quiet chat with him about his work, perhaps on the angular fragmentation on his pigment and the vitality of his patinas, perhaps not.

There can be no doubt that the young master's works will undoubtedly inspire those who are drawn strangely to such an activity but who, up to now, were too shy to demonstrate their prowess in public or who felt that they lacked the attack, flourish and intellectual message necessary.

As far as I am aware, there is only one organisation in Scotland that concerns itself with the art of graffiti. That is the Scottish School of Pure Malice and Applied Vandalism, situated at Grimness, often described as one of the holes in Scotland's central belt.

When I visited the school the other day, its principal, Dr Geronimo Groper, himself a cool, practised graffiti artist (*Second Front Now*—Edinburgh 1942, *Marples Must Go*—undated and *Free Mandela*, 1978) showed me with a touch of quiet calligraphic pride, the latest exhibition of the art to be held in the school.

Entitled *Last Writes* the exhibition is an impressive display of what young graffitists in Scotland can do when given half a chance. To say that my eyes were dazzled and my mind set a-reeling at the wonder of what I saw, would bear only a slight relation to what I really think.

Dr Groper, who accompanied me round the exhibition, showed a veteran wall writer's pride in the work of his pupils, now pointing out some work of exceptional interest, now adding or deleting some unnecessary flourish or misspelling that he felt was out of place in an establishment of such high and austere standards.

Near the entrance hall over which hangs one of the great masterpieces of pre-war Scottish grafitti, *No Sanctions against Spain* (1937), paint on billboard 12 feet by 15 feet, by R.C. Puddle, hangs a work by one of the new lads to the game: *Death is nature's way of telling you to slow up.* Executed in a lyrical, even sensuous way, and with a hint of late Gothic fantasy in the grotesque whorls of its capital letters, it delivers its philosophical message with telling impact.

The artist, Kevin Broadthirst (18), who has two previous convictions for defacement of public property and one finding of guilt for a breach of the peace while in charge of a paint spray, told me that many people had said his work had the same freshness as Hobbema and Ruisdael but he himself felt that it had more in common with the German Expressionist school. "I think a touch of Grünewald on the walls of some public building does a lot to cheer people up when life is dull and grey," he told me with a shy, disarming graffitist's smile.

Nearby is the vast: *If you can keep your head when those about you are losing theirs, you've misunderstood the situation.* By Hamish McEnemy, a well-known (especially to the police) artist, this work takes a cool, pragmatic look at the tortured world, desperately seeking some message of artistic hope and is striking in its use of mixed spray colours that produce an appropriate tartan effect always, it seems, popular in this part of the British Isles.

While I liked: *You think Oedipus had a problem. Adam was Eve's mother* by one of the few women artists. Sylvia Plank (17), (not for sale) my favourite was, *I think I exist; therefore I exist, I think,* by Ron Pindrop (21) 17 feet by 12 feet, on plaster and brick which, with its firmness of belief, mixed with equal doubt, sets up a tension that is at once keenly inspiring and charmingly baffling. Worked in canal green, rust ochre and chimney black, the graffito has already been bought by a millionaire gentleman from a certain desert land in the Middle East said to be "mad" on such forms of demotic art.

I left, gratified to see a small graffito gift on the side of my car saying: *Why worry about tomorrow when today is so far off?* and feeling that in Scotland at any rate, the paint spray is still alive and hissing and that there is no shortage of the right talent.

29

In the teeth of the Gael

AS one who has to visit the dentist at least once a year while the ravages of modern diet on his teeth are remedied and his bite equalised in strength with his bark, I read with an empathetic quiver in my back, front and side fillings that up till last month, the local dentist drill in the Sutherland port of Lochinver was operated by an ancient foot treadle.

The situation, according to our report, is to change since an American businessman, a native of Lochinver, reading of the primitive dental technology practised in that part of the Highlands, offered up to £5000 to maintain the teeth of the Gael in good condition with modern equipment. Apparently satisfactory second-hand equipment costing £1400 is to be installed that will include a high-speed, water-cooled drill with a modern chair in which patients can lean back and scream in comfort, and which no doubt will keep the teeth of local residents looking like those brushed in TV-advertised toothpastes with new miracle whiteners, stripes in the centre, flouride and other formulae suggestive of the names of new rocket fuels.

It will be a pity if the suggestion that the old drill should be placed in a museum is not carried out since its use evokes an atmosphere of an older, simpler yet more spectacular dentistry when a thread tied to an offending tooth and an ajar door was a quick and effective way to pain relief and oral health, and when the person who practised such techniques would not only remove decayed teeth but would, for a small sum, offer simples to cure warts, dandruff, bad breath as well as concocting potions to procure for ready money a wife/husband/new cow for customers or lay a blight on someone.

I have no experience of the dread treadle but in a country which now relies heavily on drills I would not have been surprised if early efforts at North Sea oil removal had used such ingenious if laborious mechanisms. The treadle operation, however, is suggestive of medieval devices used along with the rack, Iron Maiden and thumbscrew to make victims change their political or religious views or reveal where the oak chest containing the family treasures was hidden.

On the other hand, the drill, compared with some modern dental in-filling instruments, may have been reasonably painless, giving the patient only a feeling of mild judder and a dull ache extending from his back gums down to his big toes but enabling the dentist to talk easily during his work about the iniquities of the Common Market, the high price of public transport, prospects for the lambing season and the fortunes of the local football team. It may have even given the patient an opportunity to answer without making a sepulchral noise indicating acquiescence in or protest against the dentist's comments or indicating that he had only strength to yell over matters too deep and painful for him and could not give idle chat any intellectual vigour.

It may be that many residents of Lochinver have not experienced the technical trappings of modern dentistry, including high-speed, water-cooled drills or the humiliating experiences offered by the up-to-date swivelling, rising and descending dentist's chair. If so, they could be in for some moments of uncomfortable revelation that might make them wish to treadle back to old dental ways.

Until I informed him of the stark truth my dentist was firmly rooted to the belief that I scorned the use of anaesthetics to dull the pain of the drill. "You are of the older, hardier type, that made Scotland great: you are oblivious to pain, not desirous of causing more trouble than you can help to your dentist and feel proper contempt for those who insist on having such effeminate aids," he once told me.

As firmly as I could after spotting the drilling instrument in his hand I told him: "I feel pain, probably more than most people and the older I get the more of a coward I am. Jab me full of pain-killer please." Sighing as if witnessing yet another erosion of national hardiness standards and moral fibre my dentist did as I bid making me flinch and stifle a not unmanly yell as he jabbed the deadening fluid into me.

I expect that the residents of Lochinver will grit their teeth and scorn the use of anaesthetics because of pride and native resolution but if they do not, they will, I predict, find the new drills nothing to writhe home about. If they can face the steel without numbing aids they will learn immediately that the new drills sound like an over-amplified mosquito and that while they cut down the duration of the drilling they create a pitch of exquisite agony that invariably makes me—sometimes even with the use of anaesthetics—attempt to leap from the chair and grapple with my professional torturer.

The modern chair too tends to give one a feeling of unease, instability and insecurity. My dentist has a way of casually shooting me up nearly to the roof or down by his insteps—depending on what sort of operation he is carrying out—that gives me the feeling of being in a plane that is rapidly going out of control.

No dental operation, I have found, is in any way comfortable. Sometimes I have luxuriated in the process of having my teeth polished until they could temporarily blind people when the sun flashed on them.

Suddenly my dentist will stop in his work, probe at a tooth and say: "Ah, found another hole. Hang on while I drill," and before I can protest I am quivering from head to heel as the months of eating chocolate biscuits and cakes in their season catches up agonisingly with me.

Frankly I wish my dentist would give up all his modern, gleaming technology and pick up some old antique treadle drill. Then I could lie back experiencing the steady crunch of metal on some molar and getting slowly used to the discomfort without having to resort to pain-killing injections.

Then, oh then, I could explain coherently to him how I feel about metrication, the prospects for the Grand National or the 2.30 at Redcar. It might perhaps give me a feeling of being dealt with by an older, perhaps more sympathetic technology, the rhythmic action of the drill perhaps soothing me into a sleep bordering on a hypnotic trance.

"Treadle softly," I would tell him, "because you treadle on my screams." I might even look back on such experiences with pleasure. Fangs, as it were, for the memory.

30

Swelling chorus

AS the risk of incurring a diplomatic breach with the
area to the north of this column, known as Points
of View—with which I normally have the most
cordial relations—I must protest at the letter by Mr J.
Derrick McClure in which he described the children's
hymn, *Away in a Manger,* as the "dreariest thing in the
hymn book," and one with which he remembered feeling
scunnered at the age of five.

While I admit it may not be the cheeriest item in the
Christmas music repertoire that children are expected to sing
en masse, I have always had a soft spot in my affections for it
because it was one of the first choral efforts in which I joined as
a member of a mixed ability infant class with full powers to
drink, through a straw, icy and austere school milk, with the
genuine uncompromising taste of stern learning in it, making a
sound like the amplified noise of an expiring wasp.

I see the scene now as the mists of memory roll back,
revealing me, dressed like the rest of the class in a garment
supposed to represent one of the social classes in Palestine
round about the time a certain astronomical event was
taking shepherds' eyes off their flocks. Bent crowns,
amorphous cloaks, wilting artificial flowers and sagging
representations of stars on cardboard stalks, were worn or
carried by us and when we entered the school hall to belt out
our offerings, a sigh came from the audience of parents and
teachers, not so much like a great amen as of wind escaping
from a punctured inner tube.

148

All around us, on the walls, were print representations of fights for the flag such as desperate doings at Rorke's Drift in the Zulu War, the Last Stand at Battery L as Mons, Back-to-Back at Alexandria, the little-known charge of the Heavy Brigade in the Crimean War, pictures of French ships being blown up in battle, falling spars, torn sails, gunpowder smoke, flashing sabres, galloping horses, the treacherous foes fleeing from British steel and of course, many examples of the taxidermist's art, such as stuffed owls, ferrets and weasels who gazed on the assembled company with varying expressions ranging from deep cynicism to bare-teethed ferocity.

It was a curious place in which to deliver the Christmas message of peace on earth and goodwill to all men but when the toddlers let fly with their first broadside of "I saw three ships . . ." I could see women reaching for their handkerchiefs in which to bury their faces, as if the sight and sound of alleged angel infancy were too much for them, and strong men with weather-roughened Edinburgh skins, turn paler.

If that was not enough—and I often suspected it was— the defenceless adults were given *Away in a Manger,* right in the sonic solar plexus. From then on the meteorological conditions in the hall deteriorated with startling suddenness. A wave of acute seasonal depression seemed to cover the unprotected heads of the masses, heavy precipitation from tear ducts was evident and the occasional adult, broken by the sight of the children singing in flat and ragged innocence, sat with head bowed under the choral blast or managed to slip away somehow.

Since many of the children were adenoidal, teachers clung to the belief that tunes made them breathe more easily and periods in which the class sang—a loose description of the Scottish infant bellow—songs of a lively and choral nature, were many and popular. Christmas carols and hymns were taken seriously and with due respect to the music appreciation of the Great Conductor of the stars in their courses.

Once, during the bleak mid-winter and just before the herald angels were said to have sung, we were being drilled in putting on angelic expressions and singing *Jesus loves me, Yes I know*. Suddenly, through the untidy trebles of the class mass, came a voice, thin and clear, like a horn of elfland loudly piping: "and so does rag-time cowboy Joe."

I am certain that not even the last trump will erase the sound of the deafening silence that followed the words. The class gazed at each other in a wild surmise, the dancing chalk dust, whipped up by the sonic vibrations, sagged sorrowfully to the floor, and the teacher, who had stopped pounding the school piano until it groaned, cried in a voice that nicely mingled shock, agony and threat: "Who sang that?"

The culprit, the tiny heretic who flew in the musical face of herald angels and their harps, was discovered to be a little bullet-headed lad, with, it seemed, a taste for tasteless improvision.

In vain did he protest that he had learned the words at his father's elbow and assumed that they would therefore have a general adult seal of approval. He was dragged by the ear—a favourite academic way of conveying erring children for condign punishment in my day—to the headmaster, a man bowed by many sorrows, especially those relating to the evidence of unoriginal sin among young Scots.

He was not belted, but given a sound talking to within an inch of his wretched extemporaneous life; it was the scholastic equivalent of a bolt of lightning from the heavens.

Not many of us would have dared to introduce a note of loud levity in such proceedings, although some wild spirits were heard to mutter irreverent interpolations under their choral breaths. It was enough for us that we temporarily escaped the bonds of other classroom work and, for that matter, character-forming interludes in the school's Arctic-temperatured bathing pool, singing our hearts out and heads off songs from the top of the hymn, psalm and carolling pops.

The characteristic of such choral interludes was not so much sensitivity in song as a desire to make the rafters ring, the class window-panes reverberate, the electric light bulbs sway in time to our breathy blasts and to see how long our teacher could take it without slumping over the piano and sighing: "Lovely, but could we have it a little quieter the next time?"

Another teacher, almost pinned to the wall by our sonic assault, observed mordantly that he thought that in time of crisis, we could be captured the way explorers capture crocodiles—by having pieces of wood inserted swiftly between our clashing jaws.

We had just been singing *I to the Hills,* a psalm that, given the correct brio, can sound like an Edinburgh tenement collapsing in a high wind and when we slipped *O God of Bethel* into our vocal breeches and let the world echo in second accent of our barrage the teacher—a mild man, who should not have been exposed to such assaults at the chalk salient—clutched a desk for support, until, we noted, with gratification, the knuckles showed white under the strain and his lips silently mouthed the first two words of the first verse.

Other classes, we noted, had the same singing characteristics as ourselves—an unrestrained vigour and a cheerful disdain for the subtleties—if any—of melody. *Old Father Thames,* could, under favourable circumstances, bring plaster from a classroom's ceiling, *Charlie Is My Darling* was reputed to crack window-panes and if any teacher dared to toss to the glittering teeth of a singing class to worry: *What shall we do with the drunken sailor?* you could look to damage in any weak points of the building's fabric.

When we could make *Oh can ye sew cushions?* resemble an express train entering a tunnel at speed, and *Away in a Manger* sound like a cheerful charge of the Light Brigade, is it any wonder I disagree with the words of Mr McClure? "Of course not," you would say, and you would be right.

31

A Penney dreadful

I N the minds of millions of Anglo-Saxons who have
never visited the land of mountain and flood, Scotland
probably exists as a kind of selvedge of this island,
significant only in that it produces a certain ardent spirit,
shortbread, kilted regiments of a wild and uncouth nature,
Hogmanay night TV programmes of teeth-setting merri-
ment and a people who, despite their appalling health
record, are regarded in myth, legend, song and story and
vague rumour as being as tough, and at times, as genial, as
Siberian timber wolves.

The Government knows that the Scots can take it and
come up smiling, as instanced by their high incidence of
heart attacks, alcoholism, appalling housing, lung cancer
and tobacco-related diseases as well as bronchial complaints
unrelated to fags.

Their teeth are, from statistics, almost uniformly and
depressingly horrible, a bit like ancient gravestones, when
rooted in the mouth and gleam grimly when false and stuck
on with adhesives.

Their livers are in bad shape, their tongues coated and
those not suffering from bad backs are probably staggering
around with infections of the upper respiratory tracts and
inflammation on the sciatic nerve. Despite these afflications,
the Scots still go about skirling, hooting, the majority
perversely voting Labour and refusing to lie down unless
carted away feet first from pubs and funeral parlours; a
rough and often talented lot producing a couple of decent

poets, a bit heavy industry, mostly decayed, and trade union leaders with voices that could shake the foundations of Hell and shout down the great Stentor, himself.

"Scotland, where's that?" a cookhouse corporal from Birmingham, as weedy as the self-rolled cigarette that drooped from his mouth, asked me when I stood in an Army queue to get a three course meal dumped into one mess tin.

I gave the fellow the country's exact longitude and latitude, a quick version of its history and its chief imports and exports and was about to deliver a couple of stanzas from *The Lay of the Last Minstrel*—to give him the exact cultural flavour of the country—when he said: "Don't tell me, mate; I know. It's near the North Pole, it's all bog and swamp, rain and mist and beer that tastes like gnat's blood. You should cut the moorings and let the place sink."

While I didn't exactly agree with him it was neatly put. I said that, and flushed with beer and pleasure he gave me an extra helping of soup over my custard. "Better than drinking bog water, eh, ha, ha," he said.

I passed on my way, charmed by his ready wit and to this day, believe that his view of Caledonia of the bracing diesel fumes, the industrial effluent that stiffens up one's spine and the acid rain that brings a chemical flush to the cheeks is shared by many Southrons who ought to, but seem to choose not to, know better.

I expect that the late Dr W.G. Marley, of the Harwell Atomic Research Centre establishment, who in a 30-year-old paper referred to the possibility of a test explosion for an atomic device being made at a site near Wick, was one of those people who regarded Scotland—especially its northern half—as a place that was on a par with the aridity of the

Australian desert or some remote atoll in the South Pacific.

In his paper, Dr Marley said that the Wick site was unsuitable because of wetness and argued that it was difficult to keep the delicate monitoring electronics in working order "in such conditions."

Although he agreed that it would be difficult to prove there would not be a hazard to local people, the inference one might take—and I do not wish to speak ill of the departed—is that he somehow seemed just a bit more concerned for the health of the instruments rather than the local people.

In all fairness he may have been right if that was his scientific stance. Assuming that the test did not reduce Wick to picturesque rubble, detach a sizeable part of Caithness from the main land mass and deposit it in a smoking pyramid in the sea, the Caithness people, well-known to be a tough and durable lot, could probably have taken the blast in their stride.

A momentary discomfort perhaps, a certain unsteadiness on their feet afterwards, a bit of hair loss maybe and a tendency for their teeth to fall out would have been symptoms that, considering all the other afflictions that the Scots endure, would probably have gone unnoticed in the normal daily routine. They may have also had a tendency to cough a lot; but then don't we all in Scotland?

Lord Penney, described as the "Father" of Britain's atomic bomb—there's paternal pride for such a bouncing baby—said he preferred Australia for the tests and perhaps believed that the kangaroos and aborigines were even better than the Scots in coping with any resulting radiation.

I wonder; talk about the hazards of such tests may well be on the alarmist level of a Penney dreadful.

I see the average middle-of-the-road Caithness inhabitants, with no particular axe to grind, viewing the nuclear fireworks exploding overhead as being a welcome break in the monotony of their drab lives. "Bless you," I seem to hear a typical Wick housewife saying to a typical newspaperman, with an arch East Coast smile of her face: "There is nothing like a small atomic explosion to cheer you when things are dull and grey. Hardly a day goes past when some house doesn't go up or fall down. Talk about laugh!"

Even if Wick had been snuffed out accidentally—you know how Heath-Robinson some of these early British tests seemed to be—I would expect that the rest of Scotland would have gone about their daily tasks with good humour, touched and gratified in the knowledge that they had been helping the Government, the interests of which were the same as those of the country, to improve Britain's capacity to blow part of the world to smoking jigsaw-puzzle fragments.

With polonium and maybe plutonium in the air, strontium in the bones, a nice bit of crackling radiation in the breeze and atomic rain clouds overhead, the Scots could have added another interesting set of meaningful statistics to the list of their stoutly-borne afflictions that would at least give patients in doctors' waiting rooms something to talk about over the magazines.

The Scots have always been regarded by the English as extraordinarily durable, good for shoving into the imminent deadly breech in warfare and at one time for keeping the sun from setting in the British empire, the people, the old ones especially, being better able to bear the cold winter than their southern counterparts and no doubt being able to show healthy briskets to atomic tests in a way that would keel over other breeds.

On the other hand, Dr Marley, believing that such trials could be held in the UK perhaps had other areas in mind. London? Folkestone? Canterbury? We must assume so.

Dr Marley is as dead as Dicken's old Marley in the *Christmas Carol*. Perhaps if his beliefs had been acted on, many people who are in health and strength today might have been as dead as he is now. What is your opinion? A Penney for your thoughts.

32

Tea and empathy

IT is recorded—where exactly I have forgotten— that Queen Victoria, on a quiet Buckingham Palace afternoon, said to her Prime Minister, one William Ewart Gladstone, that "preaching in Britain is not as good as it was."

"Your majesty," answered the grand old man, speaking from years of political experience and worldly wisdom: "Nothing is as good as it was." That reply probably embraced *Punch,* the leaders of the *Times*, the public demand for the three-volume novel, the poetry of Tennyson, and the battle tactics of the Army's light and heavy cavalry brigades.

I doubt whether it would have included the quality of tea drunk in Britain in those days of imperial high noon when, I imagine, the stuff poured into the British digestive systems in a light-brown or milky flood with flavours ranging from the subtlest, suggesting the faint whiff of spice on a silken zephyr in Ceylon to sturdy, down-to-earth ones, hinting at the scent of boiled down Army boots and saddle leather.

The tea-tasting scene has certainly changed from those days when the tinkle of tea-cups in rooms all over this country sounded, if you had a poetic mind, like far-off temple bells on the road to Mandalay, where the dawn comes up like the colour of stewed Army canteen "char," a man can raise a thirst and where there aren't any commandments about not drinking tea out of the saucer or

159

crooking the little finger delicately over the cup handle to suggest good breeding.

According to the food critic Egon Ronay, one of the most difficult things to find in Britain is a really good cup of tea. It was now "a very rare commodity," he says in his latest publication *Just a Bite*.

His inspectors, thirsting for facts about the state of tea-making had to search all over the country to try to find a cup of tea that pleased them but the results "in otherwise excellent light meal establishments" were disappointing.

I know exactly how he and his inspectors feel. The art of good tea-making, like bespoke tailoring and good commercial bread-making is, alas, on the way to becoming as lost as the skills needed to carve and erect Easter Island statues and construct Egyptian-type pyramids.

The other day, in one of Edinburgh's leading hotels, my wife and I had a pot of tea and six small biscuits for which we were charged £2.50. I not only took exception to the price but to the tea which tasted of warm, faintly-coloured water. Inside the pot were two drowned and bloated tea-bags that even when shaken and stirred could not be persuaded to give off a flavour stronger than the distant hint of a rumour of inferior tea leaves.

Tea-making these indifferent days has been boiled down to a coarse technique; get some tea-bags and chuck them into a pot, stir if you must and gulp the stuff down as quickly as possible, preferably with some food to disguise the taste. Some establishments have the effrontery to stick only one bag into a pot for two or more people and seem genuinely surprised when indignant customers begin to show a turbulent head of complaint steam.

It is all so depressingly different from the dear dead days

almost beyond even my recall when I took part in the afternoon tea ritual in Edinburgh and when the tea came out of the pot, rich and brown like the Aga Khan, warming, stimulating and consoling, a healing influence on the bruised ego, a balm for contusions of the spirit and a producer of calm, reflective philosophies boiling down to the steamy thought that: "there is nothing so bad that a cup of tea will not improve."

In the grey light of afternoon-tea Edinburgh filtering politely through the drawn chintz curtains, only the sound of polite conversation, restrained and genteel sipping noises and the faint crepitation of cakes and sandwiches being lowered into morally-upright mouths and dealt with by rectitudinous teeth, interrupted the state of blissful, dream-like liquidity.

Outside, the traffic snarled and bayed like a beast of prey, the masses—perhaps alien and suspect coffee drinkers among them—went their dark and dismal ways but inside all was Dundee or cream cakes in their season, biscuits that matured the mind more than the greatest philosophies, and tea, ah tea, Tibetan tips, Scottish Breakfast, Earl Haig's black gunpowder, a blend of all these or maybe the usual robust and aromatic brands from the Co-op or smaller grocers that made the Scots able to face up to the rent, rates, meteorological flagellations and the general knuckle-dustered fist of fate in the small of their fortunes.

These teas were lovingly prepared, like some libation to a choosy god, the pot warmed before the tea-leaves were put in, the water itself only just brought to the boil and not allowed to bubble its nectarish Edinburgh flavour away, the correct level of teaspoonfuls used and perhaps, if you believe in the influences of orientation, the pot pointed to magnetic north when the tea was poured and the whole delicate and tender ceremony crowned by the evocative words uttered in the precise and sweetly meaningful ritual question: "One lump or two?"

Even in hotels, the afternoon tea was a ceremony of rare beauty, flecked with scones, triangled with sandwiches, crowned with cakes and the word of genteel enjoyment made liquid by tea that made eyes glaze with contentment and see clouds of glory trailing in the steam that rose from the cups.

Now, alas, such interludes are becoming rarer. Barbaric generations that, for instance, know not the taste of real fish but lust after frozen fish fingers from the fridge, and would scorn real porridge in favour of some cereal that tasted of mattress stuffing, are not likely to know or want the kind of tea that made the Scots tannin-stained empire builders, who kept the world in awe while they held as it were the nation's foes at bay with one hand and sipped their tea with the other.

With the tea we used to have, a kind of empathy was created with our fellow tea-drinkers, a temporary comradeship in cups that made us emerge from our sipping sessions restored in mind, body and spirit.

I summoned the waitress who had brought the liquid humorously dubbed "tea" to us and asked her to disclose its true nature. Could it be, I suggested gently, the effusion from some rusty boiler installed in the damp depths of the hotel, was it some kind of heated swamp water that the hotel was slyly serving as a substitute for tea as a result of a sudden shortage of supplies or was it a delicate sample of flavour-enriched Edinburgh rain gathered at great staff trouble and expense?

The girl giggled and shrugged her shapely Lothian shoulders. "Ye're daft," she said in that peculiarly Edinburgh dismissive way that has punctuated my life-long encounters with the local female sex. Perhaps I am; if so, it's probably the tea-drinking that has made me that way. With the kind of tea we get in such establishments nowadays, I am likely to regain my sanity soon.

33

A Freud in need

WHO has not heard of Professor Hans Jurgen Eysenck, controversial theorist and populariser of pyschology, has no doubt missed a great mental treat. A prolific writer, he has written some 20 books and over 500 articles in international journals, and is the author of one book that I possess called *Know your own IQ* which, when I used it to find out my proven reserves of intelligence, led to dismal results. After much application of intellect, pencil chewing, a bit of guess-work and a study of the book's examples of intelligence testing I became an expert solver of IQ problems but, I have to say, am not more intelligent.

The professor, who was born in Berlin and whose father was a comedian and mother a silent movie star—perhaps a fertile home environment for producing a child fraught with psychological problems or one skilled in wandering through the dark mental labyrinth of the human mind such as the illustrious professor—has written a book entitled *Decline and Fall of the Freudian Empire*. Since Eysenck has fiercely and frequently attacked psychoanalysis—Freud, you could say, and I might too, being a pioneer in this technique—I would take to be critical of the great Viennese mind prober himself.

Now, I don't want to cross intellectual swords with a man whose written works include *Sense and nonsense in Psychology, The causes and effects of Smoking, Genetics and Behaviour* and *I do; Your guide to a Happy Marriage,* because I fear that the outcome of his slashing, massive psychological sabre against my small piece of toy intellectual plastic, with the retractable opinion blade, would be all in that great man's favour.

Nevertheless, I do not take kindly to any attack on my friend, Sigmund—"Siggy" as I knew him in that neurosis-rich Britain before the last war—no matter how sound such attacks may claim to be.

The fact is—and I do not like to mention it but now that I am on the subject I will—that the old professor was not only a friend of my family but once, so long ago that my mind can now hardly work out whether it was a dream or in reality, he dandled me on his knee and told me, in a rich accent of old Vienna, fairy tales of a delightful psychological nature that did much to shape my character as an adult.

He, and his wife would often visit the house of my grandfather, a man of mercurial meteorological temperament, now displaying bright spells coming in from the direction of a bank balance and anon falling into a deep depression of hearing yet another speech by Ramsay MacDonald promising a Socialist paradise for Britain.

I remember, as though on an analyst's couch I lie in vacant or in pensive mood, the dark winter days in Edinburgh when the chimney smoke snuffled, groped and rubbed its back on the soot-grimed windows of the old city, when the hail bounced off the grey pavements in madcap tattoo, like the action of some nervous elemental creature in need of psycho-investigation, and when the population, bent by wind, rain, rents and rates, resembled walking Rorschach ink blot psychiatric tests.

Inside, the house, there was the cosy drawing of mental curtains and a blazing row going on, not just between

Sigmund and his friends who often dropped in for a heavy chat, but also between him and my grandfather, who had wild and whirling opinions about most things, based on very little, as well as my grandmother, who just wanted a little peace and quiet, even if it meant being put under a hypnotic spell by the professor himself.

Listen, these were good days when I was only beginning to get my first neuroses and what I believe are called intraphysical conflicts and when I used to sit symbolically at the feet of Siggy himself, listening, open-mouthed, open-minded, wide-eyed and empty-headed as the great psychopathological talks went on into the small hours with notable contributions, being made, if I remember aright, by A. Adler, C.G. Jung, A.A. Brill, Stekel and others that I hardly like to mention since my subconsious has their names buried under the ooze of Freudian slippage and I might get them laughably wrong.

Oh, how the cerebral table was pounded, the mental rafters rang with complex talk about someone called Oedipus, repressed wishes, and interpretations of dreams and the collective unconscious. Of course it was too much for my infant mind to take and I used to pluck, with a persistence unworthy of a better cause, at the sleeve of the master psychoanalyst himself as he was propounding on say, repressed impulses in the infant.

Sometimes, he would not, I regret to reveal, repress an impulse to sweep a heavy analytical hand across the back of my head, sending my mind rocking off its moorings and jumbling up my dreams for the next few nights, but often he would remove himself from the great discussion that made the window panes rattle and the flame in the gas mantle flicker and cast strange psychological shadows on the already crazy wallpaper pattern, and devote an hour or so to me, telling me tales as gnarled as old German oaks but not nearly as durable.

Even now, of a winter's night, when the wind keens between the traditional TV aerials of the city, and tugs rebelliously at the Bolshevik propaganda banners of the district council, I can recall some of the characters in his tales.

I never really understood the one Freud—or uncle Siggy as I later familiarly and familially called him—entitled Die Traumdeutung. It had, I believe, something to do with dream interpretations but was, I am told, lacking in stylistic interest, character motivation and had a poor ending, nor did Studien uber Hysterie grip me to any extent, possible because both were delivered to me in a low monotone in uncompromising German.

On the other hand, when he did speak to me in broken English which tended to sound to my pinkly juvenile ear like a car gear being noisly engaged, he could be a delightful raconteur with his stories about the never-ending, and often comic, rivalries between the ego and the id which were sometimes joined by a kind of jovial and prankish Till Eulenspeigel character called the super ego.

The super ego haunted my dreams, even the many ones I had of avarice and I often resolved to model my character and my life on it, provided other super egos that I met did not object too much.

Freud was certainly my favourite visitor, and although Jung did his Swiss best to ingratiate himself into my favour with heavy and complicated jokes about the libido, which I only pretended to understand and laugh at, I tended to treat him with icy childish reserve which his feeble attempts at hand-shadow wall symbols of the concept of the psyche as a self-regulating system, did nothing to dispel.

Adler, I could take or leave alone; I only remember that he drank tea with a piece of loaf sugar in his mouth in the Continental fashion, in a manner that resembled an inefficient pump draining a swamp.

Adler, I realise now, probably had an incurable inferiority complex, perhaps got by having to look up to Freud for too long.

Sometimes, when the world gets too much for me, when getting and spending I lay waste my powers and when I see the possibility of this little distracted globe being dissolved in flame, I wish the great good man was back with us so that he might somehow put humans on a collective couch and find out what was wrong with the species.

Uncle Freud, we need you now. Others may denigrate you; Eysenck we know better.

34

Waving palms

ONE grey Edinburgh day when I was a young reporter observing the wickedness and wiles of the world from the Press benches of the city's Sheriff Court, I was accosted, as I left that noble building of the law and, for all I knew, justice, by a local citizen badly in need of a shave, with a variety of what looked like soup stains on his tartan tie and trailing a small but affectionate cloud of flies.

"You from the newspapers, Mac?" I was asked in a conspiratorial whisper. I did not deny it; the man had instantly recognised the well-known stoop of the scribe, a bend formed by the weight of words, the burden of opinions and the continual battle against contrary winds while walking up the High Street.

The man's voice deepened. He told me that he had figured in a court case, an appearance that had caused a man of his high moral tone much embarrassment. "How much," he asked me, raising a confiding hand to his lips, "to keep my name out of the papers?"

The day suddenly brightened for me. I sensed a little harmless sport. "Fifteen shillings to keep the name out; £1 17s 6d for both name and address, an extra five bob if you—naturally enough—want your age kept out as well and for complete suppression of the story, £5 12s 9d, plus £1 to go into the editor's personal pocket and 5s to go into mine."

I could see that the man had taken my words—as they were meant—as a joke, because he laughed as in disbelief and shook his head. "You cannot," as the lines went, "hope to bribe or twist, thank God, the British journalist." I thought the point had gone home.

Conceive of my surprise when I learned later that the honest fellow had gone to our front office and offered ready cash to have the story suppressed and when sent about his business by the scandalised and blushing maidens who man, if that is the word, that part of the building, claimed he had been misled by one of the paper's minions.

Some, of course, see humour where others see it not, and from that day to this very instant, I have vowed to joke austerely and with restraint, an oath, alas, I have broken only too often.

There was one aspect of that encounter—I have had many similar ones since—that did not displease me. It was that I was considered important enough to approach with a bribe; I had, I felt, come of reportorial age. I was a force to be reckoned with, not just a person who merely filled a space that could have been used to better advantage by someone else.

According to an article in *Time* magazine, John T. Noonan, Jr, Professor of Law at the University of California, Berkeley, has written a book called—since there are no secrets between him and his readers—*Bribes*.

Professor Noonan argues that bribes have been with mankind since they dropped from trees and started commercial and political operations. He defines a bribe as "an inducement improperly influencing the performance of a public function meant to be gratuitously exercised."

The offering of gifts for reciprocal services, he says, was from the earliest times a commonplace sign of good intentions.

DRAWERS CELLULAR

Stuart Macgregor.

A roving tribesman might offer some bright stone to a stranger simply to show that he meant no violence. In Biblical stories, for instance, people were always sacrificing burnt-offerings to God, actions that in themselves could be regarded as a kind of bribe to secure divine aid or to placate the wrath of Jehovah of the Thunders.

Since then, bribery and its corollary, corruption has become a kind of monstrous octopus, occupying the minds and moistening the waving palms of grand viziers, small-time local officials, business tycoons, commercial middlemen, the upstart and the down-trodden.

Bribery stretches its grasping suckers into all walks of life where it has become run of the mill, now appearing in modern times in the realm of local and national government—and Britain is not, as one might guess, untainted—now in all echelons of commerce and anon in industry where contracts can sometimes be secured for firms by the passing of fast and underhand bucks that only stop in somebody's swollen cash balance, perhaps nestling cosily in a numbered Swiss bank account.

America, that land of free and desperate enterprise, has passed several laws to stamp out such corruption but the country, which has been rocked by the great Teapot Dome and Lockheed Corporation scandals—involving bribery on mammoth scales—still sees the well-greased palm waving expectantly for a backhander to the accompaniment of a fat chuckle and a nod that is as good as a nudge and wink.

The trouble with bribery is that many people do not think it is necessarily wrong. "Everyone's doing it, why shouldn't I get my share?" is the common excuse for pocketing a fat cheque or getting that nice little villa in Spain with a flagpole.

As some cars only hang together by the rust, so some countries are maintained solely by bribery and corruption. Take that away and the country would collapse under the weight of its moral burdens, people would lose their roots and civil unrest might take place until comfortable old corruption was restored.

As a journalist, I and my colleagues are often subjected to many forms of bribery, subtle or blatant, that can take the form of unsolicited gifts, expensive lunches by public relations officers and on rare occasions—like my Sheriff Court encounter—an offer of hard cash to write a story for the paper or keep it out. As I said, you cannot hope to bribe or twist the British journalist, but I may as well add the rest of the apophthegm, "seeing what the man will do unbribed, there's no occasion to."

When I was in the Army and held the vastly important post of quartermaster sergeant in charge of company stores in Mauritius, I was subjected to the pressure of bribery by an ancient Indian laundryman, who used to appear out of the shadows and suggest smilingly and endearingly that he would pay me vast sums of money per week—the equivalent of £5 in rupees—if I would falsify the laundry returns of the unit so as to provide a larger total than was truthful. The previous QMS had done that, I was told, so had the one before and the tradition of overblown laundry accounts was one going back to the first days of British occupation of Mauritius.

When I read nowadays of charges of laundering money being made against people, a vision of that ancient briber, appearing out of shadows that he seemed to carry with him, always rises in my mind.

When I refused his request with all the moral indignation

that a 19-year-old warrior and ex-cub could muster, and told him that it was a slice of the great British taxpayers' money that he was proposing to cut for himself and me, the old greyhead shook his head in honest bewilderment and hinted that in my khaki-drilled, puttee'd figure, the great Mauritian Dodo had returned.

Nowadays, as I have frequently revealed, governments, businesses, political parties and individuals have offered me vast sums to get even the slightest, albeit adverse, mention in this column. With such pleaders, Miss Angela Primstone, chatelaine of the columnar wine cupboard, deals firmly, "Be off with you," she says, and that, with a sigh, whimper and rustle of spurned banknotes, is just what they do.

35

Return of the fedoras

WHEN I read the news that Paul Castellano, 73, said to be the "godfather" of the US Mafia had—to use a term popular in my early film-going days—daylight shot through him, I felt that the world was probably no great loser at the fateful spilling of the gangster royal blood of a man who represented the brute forces of Neanderthal capitalism.

What was more significant to me about that grisly event was the curious dress—as if from some time-warp of the thirties—that the killers of the old king of crime had worn, described as trench coats and fedora hats.

The Mafia, it would appear, never change their sartorial fashions as they never change their basic techniques for any restructuring of their business and went out on the job wearing neatly the same garb that was de rigueur—some might say mortis—for such events as the St Valentine Day massacre in Chicago and other brisk and bustling social occasions that helped to ensure that the face of America was marred with the blackheads of endemic crime and that the statue of liberty's hand that held the torch of freedom had a symbolic greased palm.

Frankly I had forotten about the Mafia lads, my mind being taken up with little matters like 'plane and liner hijackings, IRA bombs, urban guerrillas and riots in the streets of what used to be this other Eden . . . this precious stone set in the silver sea.

If I thought of the Mafia at all, I suppose, I believed in my

175

ignorance, that their activities had lessened throughout the maturing years, that many of them had gone "legitimate" and that the old Chicago pianos, that ardent gangster-film-enthusiasts like myself knew was the nickname for the Thompson sub-machine-gun, and other arms had been hung up for monuments over the fireplace or discarded along with cement suits and concrete footwear used for rival gang disposals.

I see now that I was mistaken and that the Mafia is alive, still communicating lucidly out of the barrels of guns and spouting heavy-calibre arguments that, if competitors do not have replies ready on the tips of their triggers, can be embarrassingly difficult to rebut.

In a way they have gone respectable and possess the equivalent of boards of directors or for that matter kingly courts where those of lesser status make obeisances, where dukedoms are formed or snatched away, satrapies are created, empires built, commoners ennobled and dread lords toppled.

The Mafia areas of rule and influence exist therefore as a nation within a nation, the leering, grinning Hyde under the noble-browed, high-minded face of Jekyll, the insects who lay their eggs in the bodies of other insects to provide instant shelter, warmth and nourishment.

The names of the old gangsters resembled, in a loose sense, the lists of the knights of the Round Table, men in eternal and legendary quests for a mythical creature known as a fast buck, something almost as elusive as a unicorn.

Who does not remember the ungentle giant, spoken of in bated breaths, as "Greasy thumb" Guzik who met his end under a hail of bullets while getting the gangster equivalent of "short, back and sides," was not reading the newspapers on that day in the 1950s when American Press headlines, of a size suitable for the ending of the universe, proclaimed the presumed passage of that hulking, 15-minute-egg of a man to the great gang leader in the nether regions where seats were said to be hotter than the electric ones in Sing Sing or Alcatraz.

At one time, many a grubby mobster, with a midnight shadow on his chin, had close shaves in barber shops in Chicago and New York and paying for a trim, shave, manicure and light conversation about the declining morals of the nation, might be the signal for some supposed assistant to whip off his overalls in a theatrical gesture, take out the leveller—you would know it as a short, ugly automatic, designed to match the looks and stature of the owners—and the customer would arrive in the other world, as spruce as a newly-talcumed baby, ready for the nappy.

I was, I am not ashamed to say, brought up on a filmic diet of gangsters forever battling it out with Edgar Hoover's G-Men, the grim-jawed, slit-mouthed, clenched-teethed forerunners of the FBI in tyre-screeching car chases, deserted factories, almost specifically designed for last stands, or in bullet-pocked rooms with shattered windows and swaying, naked electric light bulbs. I once saw a cartoon in an American magazine which showed a gangster with his, if you will pardon the expression, moll, both spraying tommy-gun bullets at the police below. The proprietor in the room gazes at them with an expression of mild doubt on his face and says: "I hope you realise that no children or dogs are allowed."

While it would be wrong to say that gangsters became my juvenile idols—I had been firmly placed on the straight and slender path of the *Boys' Own Paper* and the *Childrens' Newspaper* to be swayed by the swarthy hero/villains of the screen—I did have a sneaking admiration for their entrepreneurial ways and often felt that deep down, when you got under the fedora hats, inside the leather or fur-collared coats, behind the expensive but often ill-fitting suits, you might find a lad who had a heart of sound commercial gold, whose actions were the result of an unfortunate misunderstanding between him and society. He understood that he could carry out bank raids, sell illicit liquor and hem-stitch the suitings of gentlemen with whom he had differences of opinion and society understood that he could not.

Gangsters on films, anyway, often had devoted mothers who regarded the doings of their sons with eyes misted with reproach and apprehension but when the police knocked a tattoo on their doors, with batons for manly emphasis, they would be seen at their best, placing their frail, pinafore'd, white-haired bodies between their erring offsprings and the limbs of the law, Irish to a man and built like mounds of crumbling peat, and would cry in anguish to the cameras: "You no takea my Guiseppe, Eesa good boy."

Ah, I have fought, in spirit anyway, alongside Paul Muni, scarfaced and Al Capone-ish, as he protested against insensitive policing with only the aid of a sub-machine-gun and revolvers, and a loyal female to scream encouragement at him while his besieged house was chipped away from the rones downwards by the boys in blue, watched Edward G. Robinson meet his end in a mildly interrogative way, as he stood, his weight substantially increased by an intake of best police Colt revolver lead, asking: "Is this the end of Rico?" just before the curtains descended, the credits rolled and the audience speculated idly on where to park their chewing gum.

Brave days. I thought that they had gone, like my youth too soon. Now that I know that the fedora boys have returned to public gaze, I can't wait until ardent spirits of the law put the curtains on all of the breed—I hope one day for good.

36

The lost column

SEATED at home at my word-processor I was weary but not ill-at-ease and my fingers idly strayed over the plastic keys. The fact was that after years of columnar construction, of hammering home opinions, of producing riveting prose and occasionally dropping bricks on which to produce new and shining edifices of composition, I had at last turned out the perfect column.

I gazed at the green screen—or as readers know it, the visual display unit—in a mood that was one of controlled awe and carefully-restrained satisfaction. Rembrandt, eyeing one of his newly-finished masterpieces of psychological penetration, say the portrait of Jan Six, might have felt the same way, Gibbon too, on completing the *Decline and Fall of the Roman Empire,* Isambard Kingdom Brunel on seeing the launch of the Great Eastern steamship and Beethoven, on being patted on the back by someone and told, in a mixture of congratulation and warning, after the great choral symphony had been played: "Go easy, that was one over the eight."

I looked at the column, glittering in its diamond-hard adjectives, its lapidary phrases, the richly-inlaid nominative cases and rococo adverbial-clauses, constructed in the manner of the Tsarist court jeweller Fabergé, all set against a background of royal purple prose, and I wondered where I went from there.

I was soon to know. There was a sound outside my study door and I realised that the household cat, always

Smart maying.

scratching for a living, was indicating a desire to enter, jump on my desk, sniff my work disdainfully and then move away at speed in silent, mobile comment.

Cats have a peremptory way with them and their imperatives are always to be obeyed. I opened the door, but before I did so, I switched off the word-processor to give it a chance to read, mark and inwardly digest the great work of journalistic composition that I had injected into it.

After the cat had shot a glance of deep distaste at my new adult toy and moved off to the window to look and mutter at passing cats and swear at itinerant dogs, I switched on the machine and asked it, straight, as man to micro-chip, to display the great word wonder.

It refused. It slammed an electronic door on me and derisively offered me a list of word-processing options in faraway parts of the computer of which I knew nothing and cared less. Frantically, I hammered with feverish finger-tips at various keys, seeking an entrance into the Ali Baba's cave of what we in the computer business know as software so that I could get my hands on the great columnar masterpiece. All in vain; the computer gave a smirk and kept a tight hold of it.

I spoke to that computer in its own language. A pleader of the highest forensic skill in our courts could not have done better. I informed it, in the most logical of terms, that that column might not only change the course of English literature for 1,000 years, the battle and the breeze, but might alter the path of civilisation on this planet and even have a significant influence on the intellectual development of the cosmos. Losing it would be a disaster equivalent to the burning of the library of Alexandria.

The machine considered the matter in silence. Then it

asked me what the column was headed and when told, replied that it had no knowledge of the work. It hinted that I was lying in my filled journalistic teeth. It was as I had suspected. The machine had obviously been so awe-struck by the sheer lucidity of the prose, the euphony of the word-placings, the artistic arrangements of the ideas, that it had decided—and I didn't altogether blame it—to keep the column forever.

Another explanation was that it had just got lost in the strange, Alice in Wonderland world of proportional spacing, random files, variables, double precision numbers and something, with a hint of Heath Robinson, called a middle substring.

To think with me is but to act. With one bound, I pressed a key to enable me to "search for text," and immediately I found myself in a green, throbbing electronic world looking at a signpost called "super-j script," where, if any place was suitable for my column, that would be it.

Ah, you who have not wandered, lonely as a crowd, under strange computer skies, know not the feeling of isolation and alienation a simple columnist like me can have as he blunders over a rocky landscape of templates, squelches across the plashy fields of logical expressions, where floating points move in the mental murk like a Jack o' Lanterns, and where fairy seas of forlorn intellect create waves of non-understanding on parameters of mind-bending proportions.

As I made my way through the mental mud of "soft-hyphens," my mind went back to my childhood, youth and ardent scriptic manhood when the writing life was less complicated and all a lad with a turn of phrase and a nice prose style needed for his well-being was a few sheets of paper and a typewriter that, when in action, sounded like the rattle of twin Spandau machine-guns on First World War Fokker biplanes.

My mind, dazed by the electronic landscape began to go—how shall I put it?—a little crazy and I saw myself once more back in my infant classroom, using my first writing tool, a sandbox on which I placed hieroglyphics that gave, in the tentative whorls and imperious lines, early indication of odder things to come.

Yes, I, even I, used a slate-pencil at school and even now, across the script-laden years, I can still hear the nerve-twisting squeak of these implements on the slate, that when cleaned, gave out a curious smell, the authentic scent, I always felt, of Scottish education—made up of the odour of new schoolbooks, schoolbag leather, carbolic soap, metal polish and adrenalin-stimulating fear.

As I groped my way to find a logical position somewhere on the screen, and looked cautiously at a section marked "set trap for all printer output"—something that my column had obviously fallen into and might even now be crying for help—I remembered the old pen friends of my past from the wooden, steel-nibbed ones of school that were dipped into inkpots, black as the Earl of Hell's dancing shoes, to the fountain pens that, for me, invariably leaked or ran dry just when I needed them to get someone's initials during an interview or to doodle with when reporting some boring lecture. Ah, happy days, when I hadn't a care in the world, except ink-stained fingers and people around who got the spray when I used my pen with a flourish.

I was getting desperate. I was hopelessly lost in a section marked "poke a value into machine memory," and poke though I did, nothing happened. I used all the basic keywords from "GET GOSUB GOTO, IF IMP AND INKEYS," not to mention "BASE BUFFERS" when I heard the voice of my wife. "Back in the machine again; I'll soon remedy that." There was a rattle of keys and once more I was outside and columnless and being told that I must have given the machine wrong instructions.

No matter. One day like that legendary piper who is said to have walked into an Edinburgh tunnel, got mixed up with the fairies and who might walk out again, bravely skirling and hooting so, I believe my column might some day reappear and startle everyone, most of all me. I just hope the world is ready for it; that's all.

37

For the junior activist

PARENTS who like their children's games to be meaningful and relevant to present-day world problems will undoubtedly welcome the action by Subbuteo, the table-top football game manufacturers who have introduced crowd control accessories to keep the game up-to-date.

These include police, horses, ambulancemen, stretcher-bearers and fencing for the ground. Their sales director, David Morris-Wilpred, said: "We have had requests from children to make crowds that throw toilet rolls and broken bottles but we deplore anything to do with violence and we would not do this. It is the safety factor we are stressing. The firm plan—probably not a moment too soon—to introduce crush barriers."

While Subbuteo's action is commendable as far as it goes, there are some who would say—and I am one—that it does not go far enough and that to deprive children of their inalienable right to violence might result in severe psychological damage in adulthood.

There is no use disguising the fact that football mayhem has become in a very real sense a way of life for many thousands of people, not just supporters but players and I suggest that if Subbuteo is to keep abreast of the turbulent times and maintain the realism of its game, it should also include models of casualties, emergency-operation units, blood transfusion banks, window-screen-smashed cars, houses damaged by success-maddened or disappointment-crazed fans, not to mention—but I will, because I always try to be helpful—scale models of wrecked railway carriages and terrorised railway stations.

While I have no doubt that model soldiers will always have their place in a child's garden of violence—although I have seen, and as an infant felt, the effect of dolls used by little girls as weapons—the last decade has seen shining new vistas of opportunities for toymakers to develop products that will effectively introduce young Britons to all the exciting real-life events that are going on around them every day and in which they will want eventually to participate.

According to latest advices from manufacturers' Christmas lists, stockings will be filled this year with delightfully-made toys especially relevant for the young would-be freedom fighters, street-slogan-bearers and those whose ambition is to be engaged in union meetings, industrial walk-outs, sit-ins, tooldowns and lock-outs.

Cadre Toys have introduced an impressive range of meticulously-formed and delicately-coloured lead pickets all equipped with small placards bearing relevant slogans like "What do we want?—20 per cent: What do we get— five per cent?" In the same range are boxes of plastic or metal protest marchers, some including mothers pushing prams with pop-up children, and as an optional accessory, small pipe or brass bands, also realistically moulded and cunningly painted.

Young Marxist Ltd. are to be congratulated on their Junior Picket outfit for the under-12s that comes complete with simulated industrial helmet, quilted anorak, heavy boots, small flask, sandwich case and an amusing little knuckle- duster, the latter useful when the going, perhaps with another infant wearing a board chairman's kit, gets rough.

The same firm also have a neat unisex protest demonstration outfit with large pieces of blank cardboard on which individual slogans can be written—and for the realistic touch—misspelled. The maker's suggestions, however, such as "Marples Must Go," "Heath Out" and "Second Front Now," are perhaps in need of a little updating.

Buckler & Mace, I was interested to see, have introduced a daring line in toys for the child who demands realism in his play. Their models of multiple stores which not only have nodding or dozing assistants, TV security scanning systems and customers but also shoplifters and forged note utterers of both sexes will, I am certain, make for many hours of pleasure and education.

Baskerville Press which has previously concentrated on children's political books with pop-up pictures of cabinet ministers, three-line whips and back-benchers moving private members' bills, are this year breaking new ground with their construction kits: "Build Your Own Citizens' Advice Bureau," "How to make a Race Relations Board," and "Erect an Industrial Tribunal." All kits come with relevant documents, rubber stamps, elastic bands, thread, plywood, cement, etc.

Fudlow Toys are also ahead in the relevancy stakes with a game entitled the "Bedsitter Brigade" in which players take the parts of heroic socialist workers, Communists, Trotskyists and Maoists, moving from town to town as stalwart entryists trying to take over inert, flaccid and moribund consituency Labour parties. They are opposed by evil, scheming moderate Labour fundamentalists, Tories disguised as democratic socialists and even, so meaningful is this game, by former Rhodesian sanction busters.

The same firm also has a multi-coloured 25,000-piece jigsaw puzzle showing the face of the real Labour Party. After working at it for three hours, I was unable to complete the picture and I found it and I expect many children and those who are infants at heart will do so as well—a disappointing and baffling exercise.

Books? Plenty of them this year, many simply riddled with relevancy to this day and age. Every child will surely love: "My Very First Freedom Fighter and Urban Guerilla Manual," by Brigadier Che Braganza, formerly on the staff of the Cuban War Office (Trotskyhurst Press, £5.75).

Fully illustrated with pictures and diagrams it gives a thumpingly-good grounding in the latest guerilla techniques including weapon training, the use of mortars, flame-throwers, mess tins and the button stick. There are excellent sections on anti-tank weapons, how to arrange an ambush, dig anti-personnel traps, sabotage industrial complexes and information on how to take stones out of tank tracks and on which side of a tree moss grows.

Another corking book to be commended is: "TUC Conference O' My Heart" (Left Wing Yarns, £4.05), in which the heroine, a beautiful young Marxist and women's lib ecologist, meets a handsome, free-fisted, motion-moving engineering union shop steward and how socialist love flowers amid a background of bitter party divisiveness, inter-union feuds, scabbing, blacklegging and endless near-lethal motions on the suspension of standing orders.

Mainly for girls, this book is nevertheless a sound technical manual for young activists of all sexes in that it devotes many chapters on how to move motions, points of order, amendments to points of order as well as addendums and vice versa.

Lastly, "My Own Socialist Colouring Book" (Zinoviev

Press, £3) is highly suitable for under-eights who will spend happy artistic hours colouring well-known Labour personalities including their many properties over the country and their bank balances. I confess, I enjoyed doing it myself.

38

Casting the clout

"NE'ER cast your cloot (clout) before May is oot (out)"—well-known Scottish wise saw and modern instance.

The day for the big sartorial event of my summer dawned bright and clear with no sign of an occluded front, a fall in the barometric pressure or even the faintest hint of a Northeast wind edging in from the sea and equipped, as is usually the case, with the meteorological equivalent of an open razor and bicycle chain.

Since it does not do to make drastic changes in one's clothing because of the acknowledged fickleness of Edinburgh's climate, I had been adapting myself gradually to the big deciduous day by making small, barely perceptible changes in my garb.

In February, for instance, I put on a lighter type of shoelace and because I regard myself—against all evidence to the contrary—as one of Scotland's hardy sons I braced myself in March to dare the worst the weather could throw at me by discarding my heavy-duty, thorn-proof, rain-resistant tweed tie for one of lighter texture.

April, laughing her girlish laughter, saw me discard the fireproof, insect-repellent detachable inner-lining of my overcoat, a garment assembled rather than stitched together to defy all the elements including Antarctic blizzards, monsoon rains and hot desert winds.

May saw me go over, as a concession to the swing of the seasons, to rubber heels on my shoes instead of winter-quality leather and on that month, although I knew I was taking a risk that I might regret instantly, I took off my foul weather cuff-links and replaced them with ones of lighter weight suitable for informal summer lounging in holiday hotels watching through the aspidestra leaves the rain beating on the window panes.

June is the month I traditionally and cautiously acknowledge that summer might be with us, when I shed my winter clothing weight and emerge into the sunlight, blinking and ready to retreat at the first sign of shock—like a hermit crab emerging from its protective shell.

I come from a long line of ancestors who regarded the weather with maximum suspicion and who protected themselves against the elements with several layers of clothing, the general effect making them look like small, waddling, armadillos, perspiring heavily in winter's heat and feeling snug in the high chill of June, the cooling downpours of July and the piercing winds of August.

As a schoolboy, I was afforded the stoutest type of clothing that money and Provident cheques could buy. I had school caps that could survive 1,000 years the battle and the breeze, clothbadged jackets that could withstand sooty rain, blizzards, inked pellets and being used to mark goal areas in unofficial games of football, woollen stockings with school colours that, despite the fact that when garterless they obeyed the force of gravity and concertina'd, at least nullified the demoralising and perhaps lethal effects of high winds playing around sensitive ankles, and shoes built to a design and durability that suggested they were conceived by naval architects on the lines of the early dreadnought battleships.

Oh, yes, furious winter could rage, spring and summer

DREADNOUGHT SOCKS

WARM TIES

THORNPROOF TIES

Stuart Macgregor.

too and if autumn wanted to get in some equinoxial skullduggery, that could be handled as well with double-knit, reinforced-gusseted, super underwear suitable for growing boys and girls of a delicate constitution, heavy school rain-coats that felt as if they could have withstood shrapnel, and school pullovers of a thickness that immediately made the wearer sag at the knees with fatigue before he had taken even one shaky step in his ironclad footwear.

The Army also took the view that its male personnel should be protected heavily from sudden days of chill or unexpected heat by clothing them in garments of unbeliev-able thickness from battledress to underwear which looked and felt as if they could stop a 4.7 inch naval shell in mid-trajectory. Even my forage cap was heavy and hairy and from a distance looked like a small animal perched nonchalently on the side of my head, a resemblance that drew much aggrieved comment from NCO's.

On parade on a summer day, each man was like a mobile furnace emitting steam from any gap in his uniform and on parade it was sometimes as good as a play to see the domino effect of one man toppling against another as he succumbed to the heat while the temperature inside the regimental sergeant major's uniform rose a couple of dangerous degrees and his face assumed the puce colour of the sky before the onslaught of a typhoon.

There were times—ah how the shiver of remembrance shakes my body like the ague—when, throwing caution and winter clothing to the winds I would don summer garb before the month of May was out not believing the perils that awaited the foolhardy who exchanged heavy overcoats for ones of lighter weight or—even more daring—did not wear a coat at all and flaunted themselves in the face of malevolent fate by wearing open-necked shirts.

How confident such persons would be striding in the hot morning streets of Edinburgh little knowing that by the afternoon, the day would have taken on a steely tinge and that by evening the first fringes of the North Sea mist would have crept into the capital making people feel, in the depressing greyness, that winter had returned. Then people would blow a nose, the first hint of sinusitis would appear and in others the premonitory tickle in the throat or chill in the bones would echo past colds and presage ones to come.

Since glorious June is here, the weather appearing clement at least for a few days, I decided that it was the time to hold the Morris casting of the cloot ceremony by tradition held in the first few days of the month assuming that I am in good enough health and in possession of sufficient strength to stand the shock of shedding winter garments.

"Are you sure you are ready in mind and body for this?" asked my mother who had an emergency bottle of cough linctus and a double-strong catarrhal lozenge standing by in her medical cupboard while my wife rushed to shut all windows in the house and turn up the central heating so that the trauma of changing to summer wear should not be too great.

I took off my tie and cautiously opened my shirt by one button at the neck. So far, so good, no sudden chill had hit me. I removed my pullover, my trusty shield and comforter in the worst that winter could throw as me. "You're going too far," gasped my mother, "at least wear a chest protector."

I shook my head bravely, making my hat fall off. I left it on the ground. "Not that," said my wife paling, "you can't go without your hat, it's part of you like your ears, your wallet."

With a light laugh that had just the trace of laryngitic hoarseness in it, I brushed her fears and my remaining hairs aside and donned my light Tunisian tweed jacket with the Taiwanese semi-tropical-weave trousers.

With confidence in my heart, the breeze on my head, just a hint of gooseflesh on my skin and a rumour of panic and disarray in the inevitably troubled region of the upper respiratory tract, I strode into the treacherous summer air.

At times a man must— excuse my sneezing—live dangerously.

39

Museum peace

AS a museum lover I must take issue with Mr Michael Montague, director of the English Tourist Board who the other day described British museums as "very tame, very dull and very boring." Some which did enjoy fame in London, he said, did not deserve it. Museum curators, he added, with what justification I know not, were "even duller, pompous and crusty."

He made the remarks as he presented a £250,000 cheque for Britain's newest museum, the futurist Viking centre due to open in York next summer.

The £2.5 million underground Jorvic Centre, built on the site of the original Viking town, incorporates a science fiction time capsule. Visitors will see the town as it stood 1,000 years ago and will, in a curiously anachronistic form of travel, be transported through it in electric cars while noises, pictures and even smells of the period are projected by audio-visual technology.

Mr Montague said it would be "the finest museum in England when it opens and a challenge to others to surpass it."

This space-age development leaves me, a museum traditionalist, as cold as the stares one sometimes gets from attendants who suspect you of dishonestly handling a Mesozoic or early Cambrian fossil or of breathing heavily on the glass cover of a case containing Melanesian sea shells.

I admit, though grudgingly, that audio-visual displays and other types of modern, visually impactive presentations have their place in museums to pander to the fickle and easily pleased tastes of modern visitors, but they must not be allowed to dominate and turn a museum into a kind of informative fun fair.

There should be, I submit to any museum planner or administrator who might read this, areas of quietness— some who know no better might say dullness—where a visitor can wander in a hypnotic museum dream; where he can stare, as through a dusty glass unclearly, at, say, a stuffed, tooth-bared, eye-glaring caracal lynx and let himself enter into deep philosophical thoughts about the transitory nature of life and maybe about the very stuff of the universe itself.

I equate the atmosphere of the museums I have known and loved since childhood with that of certain Victorian swimming baths—dark, quietly contemplative, faintly mysterious, with a kind of perpetual twilight glow about them, where the solemn, even respectful, atmosphere is broken, in the case of museums, by the occasional cry of delight from some enraptured visitor who sees, perhaps for the first time, a stuffed reticulated python gazing with every indication of reptilian distaste at the taxidermist's triumph of a charging wildebeeste or a Grant's gazelle.

I like to drift about museums, perhaps near closing time when attendants' arches ache and cafeteria staff brush the hair out of their eyes in a queenly way to mark the end of their toil.

Then, the low hum of working models of early steam clocks, horseless carriages or 1922 locomotives sound like the far-off, barely-heard lament of fog-horns. The seabirds of the West African coast take on a distinctly bright-eyed, sharp-billed and menacing look, and the Egyptian room, with its replicas of sarcophagi, mock-up of mummies, and sepia-tinted photographs of the Sphinx and the appropriate pyramids takes on a curious air of brooding and remote antiquity such as one might experience in some kingly burial place in the fabled land of the Nile itself.

I remember reading some years ago that stuffed animals in Exeter's museum, some of them over 50 years old, were to be destroyed in the "interests of scientific accuracy." Time, sunlight and moths had apparently transformed their coat texture and natural colouring into what scientific perfectionists considered a travesty of the real thing.

I have been in museums, small and obscure ones certainly, where creatures of rich and strange colourings unknown to natural historians existed decayed hoof by bedraggled tail, yellowing tooth by broken claw; where stuffed deer had their coats apparently reddened with boot polish, hedgehogs had turned a curious orange colour—perhaps by the over-use of dyes—and pygmy elephants and other creatures had been changed subtly over the years into fantastic creations by the steady work of local mice and termites.

These creatures had a strange fascination for me, since they might have existed in fanciful illustrations of Mallory's Arthurian legends. I have spent many happy hours letting my imagination work on some purple-coloured walrus, pink British squirrels and a Bengal tiger, perhaps turned green by verdigris, whose unnaturally bright yellow eyes seemed to follow the visitor everywhere.

Ah, the long, dream-like hours I have spent in such places of almost holy quiet, walking along dim corridors lined with green Victorian bottles, rooms with faded and indecipherable maps, ancient pieces of metal-work attributed to job creation schemes among certain Caledonian tribes and suits of rusty and ill-fitting armour. In corners sat ancient attendants with faded medal ribbons on their jackets, nodding on their hard chairs and occasionally jerking awake to fix the visitor with a glaring accusatory eye.

I have been in small towns in Britain where some elderly and benign curator had to be roused from sleep in his house to open the door of the nearby museum or where some housewife-museum-minder would dry her dish-washing hands on her apron, hand over the key with a smile and express the hope that you enjoy the visit.

These are the places where one can muse properly over the collection of local flint arrowheads, the town's first mobile fire pump, photographs of the cricket team bearded and scowling at the world, a collection of officers' trouser-presses that once belonged to the local fencibles, shell cases from the First World War, an early town telephone and the vestigial remains of what might have been a sandal of a Roman centurion.

In none of these places did one get the strident and peremptory voice and camera-whirr of audio-visual equipment, which gives some visitors the feeling that they are being dragooned into information, perhaps more that they need at that moment.

I have never thought Edinburgh's Royal Scottish Museum, the National Museum of Antiquities or any of its other museums tame or dull and I have been ever a happy visitor to those in Glasgow and other parts of Scotland.

Should any of them introduce audio-vision into their buildings, other than in a discreet and tasteful way, you will find me and people like me not slackening in their enthusiasms for these places, but keeping well away from the sight and sound. We will lurk, with every indication of contentment, among remaining collections of faded tropical moths, models of early heavier-than-air machines, silhouettes of local dignitaries, collections of Victorian moustache cups and faded and yellowing ant-eaters.

As I gaze abstractedly at figures forever sporting on some Grecian urn, savour the all-pervading educational gloom of some museum strong on quietness but perhaps somewhat weak on scientific approach. I know that I shall not miss absenting myself from the new York museum.

In any case, from what I know of the Vikings, the sounds and smells of that period are hardly what a refined and sensitive museum-goer like myself would care to experience. Once, when in a run-down but still charming little museum on the Welsh border near Shrewsbury, an ingrate of a visitor remarked: "This place ought to be in a museum." In my view he had paid it the highest compliment of all.

40

Send in vainglorious

I take it that in Scotland, a national-anthem-conscious nation, most people are familiar with the anthem of Rwanda, a tuneful republic in central Africa which has knocked up for itself, perhaps with tom-tom and nose flute accompaniment, a rhythmic little number designed to produce a catch in massed throats, a swell in the pride and maybe a tear in the eye.

There are four verses but for reasons of space I will quote only the third which captures the spirit of the melodic compliment to the nation and its political, economic and territorial aspirations.

"Home born Rwandans all, beat the victory drums! Democracy has triumphed in our land. All of us together we have striven for it arduously. Together we have decreed it— Tutsi Twa, Hutu with other racial elements. This hard-won Independence of ours. Let us join to build it up. Let us cherish it in peace and in truth, in freedom and in harmony."

While it may lack a certain clearly-stated pride in the unique beauty of the land, a hint that heaven regards it with a favourable eye and that its people can hope for divine protection in the event of any incursions by oppressing foreigners, the anthem follows much the same formula as those for other national inspirational pieces. It is composed to keep the country not just in melodic chorus but firmly in step in the march of the nations, most of which are no doubt bellowing their own anthems extolling the virtues of their people, the scenic wonder of the land and that God is, or certainly ought to be, on their side.

As it is written and, I have no doubt, sung, the Rwandan anthem is, in my opinion, no worse and certainly no better than say, "God Save the Queen," the "Star-Spangled Banner," that of Soviet Russia and for that matter all the other vainglorious, pompous and chauvinistic pieces of music that are intended to symbolise a nation and which go with fluttering flags, artillery salutes, presenting arms and fainting guardsmen.

It may well be fit to be played firmly, and for all I care proudly, alongside—at the same time if necessary—the latest attempt at an anthem for a Scotland which is apparently cruelly suffering from anthem deprivation, the words by the poet Alan Bold and the tune composed 35 years ago by Francis George Scott.

I have not heard the melody and therefore cannot comment on its inspirational qualities and whether Mr Bold's words combine well to make an anthem that will stir the Scots as if by a bugle, will draw old men from the chimney corner, young men from the video, pub and dartboard and children from igniting schools and vandalising public 'phone kiosks, but from reading the verses as printed in *The Scotsman* yesterday, I do not feel they will make the fair-to-average Scot swell with quiet or rowdy melodic and national pride.

There is a kind of cryptic quality in the words that might make people pause before making a rugby or football ground echo to them. "Scotland, Scotland, gather as a clan," is one line. And then what? We know what clan gatherings often led to in this embattled land—rape, murder, fire and, according to authoritative historical sources, the sword.

The lines: "Now the country is a nation alive to itself and the chorus sweeps forward in time" seems to me, I must confess, somewhat baffling and may be so to many other people who genuinely feel that an anthem is vital for Scotland's spiritual well-being and that until it has one the country will not be able to lift up its head among anthem-rich nations like Gabon, Honduras or Haiti—the last country having the lines of one verse: "For flag on high, for native land, 'Tis fine to die. Our traditions demand. Be ready, heart and hand, 'Tis fine to die, 'Tis fine to die. For flag on high for native land."

I do not wish to be unduly carping about Mr Bold's effort because I do not think it matters a dactyl to an iambic pentameter, a line about sacred soil to another about flag and glory what his verses signify because, apart from some notable exceptions, most anthems are, in my view, so much melodic and versifying fustian that could be easily interchanged from one country to another with the population hardly noticing or caring.

I have before me a book entitled *National Anthems of the World,* lent to me through the courtesy and efficiency of Edinburgh Central Library's music section, and a study of it makes dismal reading.

From the contents one could knock up a global anthem by stringing key phrases together and setting them to an appropriate tune of nobility, say that of "Ten Green Bottles Hanging on the Wall."

Such a work would be sternly imperative and demand that the deity saves the world from its foes and all misfortunes, spiritual, economical, geological and political. Its theme will be the defeat of despots, the breaking of fetters, the freeing of the people, the scattering of tyrants, telling the world that dawn is at hand and that the earth will be made a cradle of noble heroes. "March on, march on. Forward, conquer or die.

"All hail... May justice be our shield... O fair Madagascar... God Bless Malawi... Preserve Equatorial Guinea... God be with our Surinam." So it goes on... "Save the Queen, confound our foes, bless those in authority in Swaziland, down with oppressors and up with the flag.

Most national anthems depress me and when I have to stand for them I get not just an ache in my back, but a pain in the neck and sag in the spirit.

Although I cannot believe that a national anthem is necessary to maintain levels of pride and confidence in the future of and respect for the past of a country, there was a time when I, even I, would stand unwavering along with the rest when Britain's national anthem came on in cinemas.

I maintained that firm stance when the dastardly crowds used to rise as one man and attempt to leave even while the anthem was playing. I used to turn myself into a small obstacle on my aisle, blocking the massed escape from homage and at times indicating that people should return to their seats and stick it out like true Britons.

I remember a London music hall turn in my boyhood in which a faintly-alcoholic-looking gent with full evening wear came onto the stage and said: "Little patriotic recitation... Oh Engerland is Engerland still. It always was and always will. Though foreign foes may brag, we love our dear old flag and Engerland is Engerland still...."

Then he got off somehow, the audience clapped sporadically and shifted their old English humbugs from one cheek to another until the comedians came on.

If this country does need an anthem, I suggest one with topical relevance such as: "Hail Caledonia with general precipitation moving in on an occluded front from the Azores, we pallid stay-at-homes and sunburned exiles salute thee. Scotia, land o' cakes, fish fingers and the knuckle sandwich, we raise our foaming tankards of chemical beer and packets of traditional crisps like granny made in her little grey Heilan home in the west to toast you and ask with heartfelt thankfulness: "Wha (in the vernacular) is like us? Heaven help Scotland and quickly we cry and if the four corners of the world come towards us we will shock them with our hotel prices. Hail Caledonia, etc . . ."

41

Money talks

T HERE was a time—in my case it was roughly
around the period when "meadow, grove and stream,
the earth and every common sight, to me did seem
apparelled in celestial light"—when to travel outside the
British Isles marked one as a person of enviable financial
resources, leisure and luck or who had the kind of job that
took one to the lands of palm and pine, mosque and
mosquito, prickly heat and fevers of the dengue, tick and
blackwater varieties.

These voyagers were often a great source of admiration
and speculation to those who never had an opportunity or
the money to visit those amorphous sections of the world
known as "abroad." They were people who had breathed
the dusty classical air of Pericles and Aristotle and had been
stung by sand-fly and taxi-driver in the land of the
pharoahs, had seen the sun set an empire red on rickshaw
operators on the waterfront of Singapore, had actually
walked down odoriferous, noisy and many-bodied
thoroughfares with names like the Street of a Thousand
One-legged Sand Dancers and were people whom hyenas
had sniffed at and had slunk away cowed by the scent of
freshly-laundered British khaki drill.

When they came back to these crowded islands, where
the majority of the population got no further on their travels
than the nearest sea-side resort or country holiday
settlement spiky with baronial-type hotels or boarding
houses named "Dunrovin" or "Bide-a-Wee", they were in

great demand to give side-show talks on "A Traveller in Spain." "A Businessman's View of Bali" or "Sunny Days in Sicily."

At school, I had a geography master who had been to Japan. Think of that! Land of the lotus blossom, geisha girls bearing scented tea and warriors swishing the air with curved, artistic, suicide swords.

He never revealed his experiences but to whet pupils' expectancies he would say "One day, I will tell you about my travels in that fabled land. Meanwhile turn to page 60 in your geography books—imports and exports of Paraguay—and memorise the page as I shall question you about the contents later."

Among the glamour figures of the twenties and thirties and even into the early sixties were foreign correspondents of newspapers who could write: "I was the first journalist to enter shell-torn, bullet-riddled, fly-blown El Garish."

They conjured-up images of intrepid writers, rattling off staccato bursts of impactive prose as bullets nicked their eye-shades, shrapnel peppered their massed expense account sheets and the occasional bottle of field service gin was shattered by sniper fire.

Somehow the romance of strange-sounding places with far-away names has faded and the number of people who have been abroad—some to places that were once the haunts of the most daring travellers—grows yearly until it seems that just about everyone in Britain has drunk tea like mother made in some resort on the rim of the Mediterrean basin, has eaten fish and chips among the concrete and glass glories of some Spanish costa and disco-danced until the night sagged and morning cracked in the penumbra of the Parthenon or the shadow of the Shwe Dagon pagoda where the old flotilla lay and the photogenic dawn came up like thunder out of China cross the bay.

The fading began in the early sixties when package tour operators began shipping people *en masse,* like container cargoes, to hotels abroad which processed them into a holiday in the way that peas are canned. By that time, of course, people were able to spare money from the purchase of crusts of bread and a bone to mumble over and were open to allocating cash to sit in cafes in Ostend and eye the natives suspiciously or set a cautious foot into dancing, drinking, castanet-clicking, Spain.

I can remember telling people around 1951 that I seemed to be among the first British tourists to enter wine-sodden, fly-biting, native-haggling, street-thieving San Verez-Anne where I had enjoyed the local amenities such as deep glasses of the blushful Hippocrene with intricately-beaded bubbles winking at the brim and taken part in traditional activities such as trying to cope with the subsequent headaches as well as dealing with local variations of North African Tum.

People regarded me with the same awe as those who beheld the Jumblies coming home after going to sea in a sieve. They marvelled at the sights I had seen, the dangers I said I had overcome and wished they had had the courage and the money to go abroad and face up bravely to the shifty and untrustworthy natives who might live anywhere from Dusseldorf to Dar-es-Salaam. Now, I could have a holiday on an ice-floe sailing out from the Arctic and returning to Britain via the Gulf Stream and nobody would roll an eye or bat a lid.

The other day when I was having my hair cut, the assistant revealed that he had just come from a world cruise. "The wife and I just thought we'd give ourselves a little treat that would make a difference from the usual holiday we take every year in the Bahamas. Never been to the Bahamas, or on a world cruise? You should sir, travel, they say, broadens the mind."

As he snipped the petrified forest of my hair. I reflected moodily that at one time that lad would probably have been content to take a week at Rothesay or Crail and consider these places almost in the light of voyages to Ultima Thule.

While travel no doubt broadens the mind it also thins the wallet and these days I tend to wander about in a light daze of speculation at the amount of money people appear to spend on their holidays.

"Yes, been to Greece in April," said the chap behind the bar of an Edinburgh hotel to me the other day, "going down the Nile in October and maybe, if the wife and I feel like a break to get us through the winter, we might go to Spain in January."

Where, I ask, as I pay my latest household bill in order to exist on this expensive earth, are they getting the money from? Here, I will speak to a garage hand who has just got himself a flat in Spain, there a window cleaner who has just bought a bungalow in Madeira, and anon a bus driver who is toying with the idea of getting "a little place in Portugal where we can stay on holiday or let it out to tourists."

I met a friend the other day. "Just going off to Australia for three months," he said—just like that. "When we come back we might go to our cottage in the Dordogne for a week or so or we could take a cruise up the Ganges. You're going where? The Lake District? For the rain-tasting? Oh well, it takes all sorts."

Yesterday, I met a fellow who has been out of work for about a year. "Just flying off to sunny Minorca for a few weeks," he revealed. I sat down with the shock and brooded for a bit in cloudy Edinburgh.

I am told that money talks. I wish it would talk to me for a bit, I'm a good listener.

42

I am a wrong number

DID you know that if you are dissatisfied with your standard telephone you can, as a result of the inventive genius of British Telecom, buy others from a selection of 18 special 'phones which include ones shaped like Mickey Mouse and Snoopy, the old type of daffodil-shaped instrument and others, modernistically-styled, with names like Rhapsody and Contempra?

As a 'phone user for whom the bell tolls regularly I wish that British Telecom could provide a 'phone for wrong number holders because that is what I am apparently shaped by fate to be for the rest of my telephone subscribed life.

People are very adept at identifying my wrong numbered status when I answer my 'phone. "You are not Harry," a female voice said on my 'phone the other night after I had picked up the shrill-sounding instrument. I confessed, with a manly frankness that her assertion was correct. "Then what are you doing answering the 'phone?" the voice said. Before I could explain and apologise, the voice said accusingly: "You're a wrong number, that's what you are," and hung up.

Well, I admit it; why should I try to hide the fact? The mark of the ether annoyer is on me and I know, deep down in the heart of my instrument, that no matter what number I have, whether it is one indicating the illustrious suburb of Edinburgh's Newington or that of some adjoining district, equally admirable, my number will be one that draws unsuspecting 'phone callers to dial it with disappointing results for them and a reaction that varies from polite tolerance to testy impatience from me.

Discovering that one is a wrong number is often a dispiriting experience, perhaps akin to finding out that one's ancestors were sheep stealers or responsible for some shady trade in selling guns that squirted fire water to Red Indians.

I found out my numbered wrongness very early in my 'phone renting life when one of the first calls I received on my new instrument was from a young girl who seemed baffled when I announced my number in tones of restrained pride. She asked hesitatingly: "Is . . . er . . . that Daphne?" In my deepest bass baritone voice that has been known to send reverberations around the house, let alone the bathroom, when I break into my rendering of "Down Among the Dead Men," I told her that I was not Daphne and that no person answering to that name was in our household or ever likely to be.

"I must have dialed a wrong number then," the caller observed brightly. There was a click, a whirr and I was left to contemplate the full significance of her remarks. A wrong number? Me? And I was only 25 too and up to then life had seemed smooth and straightforward for me and full of the promise of glorious telephonic sunny uplands with untold heaps of correct numbers coming onto and going from my 'phone and not one hint of digital inexactitude.

Immediately I felt as if I had something like the mark of a pariah on me, a feeling that was emphasised a couple of nights later when I picked up the 'phone and had to tell the caller that he had got his digits slightly mixed. "Oh all right then," he said huffily. A couple of minutes later the 'phone rang again. It was the same caller. "You still have the wrong number." I said patiently. "Are you sure?" the man asked, adding that he was certain he was dialling correctly and hinting that I might as well admit he was right and produce a Mr Grierson alleged to be in my house. I assured him that his suspicions were groundless and he hung up.

Shortly afterwards the 'phone rang again. It was the same caller. "You again," cried the voice. "You've still got a wrong number," I told him. "If you're a wrong number, you shouldn't answer," was the response followed by the sound of the receiver being slammed down.

There you have the quintessential problem of the wrong number holder. He knows that if he answers the shrill summons of the bell he could annoy some innocent caller who might ask him if he would like to come to the theatre next Wednesday week because she (the speaker) had been given two tickets for a theatre and that she would not take any excuse like washing hair that night or shortening a pair of jeans for non-acceptance of the offer.

It is no good the wrongly-numbered saying he would love to come, that he had very little hair to speak of, that it could be washed in about three minutes flat and that he never wore jeans, only tweed suits of a particularly hairy and durable character. If he is not Simon or Nigel or whoever the caller wanted, his words are usually received in stony silence or a polite "No thanks."

Not so long ago my phone rang with peremptory clarity, just as if I was a right number, which I must confess I am at times. When I picked it up, a voice said: "Well?" I told the caller I was, that I had passed a comfortable night and that there was every hope that I might stagger on in this uncertain world for a bit longer. I thanked him for ringing and said no further bulletins were being issued about my health. "Who is that?" the voice asked in tones that suggested ill-suppressed bafflement.

I revealed to him that I was Albert Morris, the well-known wrong-number, all callers politely redirected. "Oh, I though you were my girl friend. I wanted to know whether she had made up her mind to come on holiday with me. You know how it is?" I said I didn't and we both hung up, each no doubt speculating on the interesting class of people you meet when wrong numbers are dialled.

There are, I know, along the vast telephone network other wrong numbers. I get on to them inadvertently and feel the gratification that an astronomer would experience if he had managed to contact some other apparently intelligent civilisation in the galaxy.

Recently I made a 'phone call and found that I had dialled a wrong number. The woman at the other end of the line cheerfully accepted the fact. "I wanted to speak to my aunt," I told her. "Well I'm an aunt, won't I do?" she asked. Regretfully I said that I could not fully accept her as a substitute but I did speak to her on things in general for a few seconds and we hung up with mutual expressions of goodwill.

Being a wrong number is a state that at least is one of interesting uncertainty. You never know who will 'phone you but you can always be sure that it will generally be when you are about to step into or are settled nicely in your bath, when you are poised to make a precision sweep with your razor, you have just sat down to a meal, you are about to have a light post-lunch doze, have fallen asleep at night or have just left the house but can hear your 'phone ringing 30 yards away.

Sometimes I wish the wrong numbered—who cannot help other people dialling them—could form a club and discuss their experiences and maybe get technical and spiritual experts to show them how to adapt to their plight and especially how to overcome the curious flat feeling they get when they find out they they have long periods of being boringly correct numbers.

I wish, most of all, that British Telecom would add a "wrong number" 'phone onto their models range which would, by some method of electronic and telepathic osmosis, cut wrong-number diallers off or only let through those who might have some spiritual affinity to those who wrongly received the call.

Or am I asking too much?—Surely not!